the
PRINCE
BOOFHEAD
SYNDROME

Michael Carr-Gregg is a child and adolescent psychologist, broadcaster, a well-respected speaker and one of Australia's leading authorities on teenage behaviour. In 1985 he founded CanTeen, the acclaimed cancer patients' support group for teenagers in New Zealand and Australia. He is the consultant psychologist to many schools and national organisations, and has written eleven books on parenting adolescents.

Elly Robinson is a researcher, writer and mother who began her career as a youth worker. Since then she has worked to promote the use of evidence in practice with children, young people and families. She has a Graduate Diploma in Adolescent Health and a Master of Public Health from the University of Melbourne.

BOOKS BY MICHAEL CARR-GREGG

Surviving Adolescents

Real Wired Child

When to Really Worry

Surviving Step-Families

Beyond Cyberbulling

Strictly Parenting

The Princess Bitchface Syndrome 2.0
(with Elly Robinson)

the PRINCE BOOFHEAD SYNDROME

DR MICHAEL CARR-GREGG
AND ELLY ROBINSON

PENGUIN BOOKS

PENGUIN BOOKS

UK | USA | Canada | Ireland | Australia
India | New Zealand | South Africa | China

Penguin Books is part of the Penguin Random House group of companies
whose addresses can be found at global.penguinrandomhouse.com.

Penguin
Random House
Australia

First published by Penguin Random House Australia Pty Ltd, 2017

1 3 5 7 9 10 8 6 4 2

Cover design by Alex Ross © Penguin Random House Australia Pty Ltd
Text design by Louisa Maggio © Penguin Random House Australia Pty Ltd
Cover photograph by Shannon Fagan/Dreamstime.com
Typeset in Adobe Caslon by Louisa Maggio, Penguin Random House Australia Pty Ltd
Colour separation by Splitting Image Colour Studio, Clayton, Victoria
Printed and bound in Australia by Griffin Press, an accredited ISO AS/NZS 14001
Environmental Management Systems printer.

National Library of Australia Cataloguing-in-Publication data:

Carr-Gregg, Michael, author.
The prince boofhead syndrome / Michael Carr-Gregg and Elly Robinson.
9780143784272 (paperback)
Subjects: Teenage boys.
Parent and teenager.
Adolescent psychology.

Other Creators/Contributors:
Robinson, Elly, 1968- author.

penguin.com.au

Contents

Introduction

A few years ago I was standing outside my son's school early one morning after dropping him off. I'd just finished texting a work colleague about some urgent matter when a four-wheel drive pulled up and a glamorously dressed and beautifully coiffed woman got out, clutching a folder. She stood a few metres away, pulled out a smartphone and tapped out a text message. A few moments later a short, skinny boy in school uniform sauntered up to her. 'Here it is, darling,' the woman said, proffering the folder to the boy, who was clearly her son.

The schoolboy, not more than 13 years of age, took one look at the folder and said loudly, 'That's the wrong one, you stupid hag! I needed my *maths* folder! Now I'm up shit creek and it's all your fault.'

The woman looked close to tears as she stuttered, 'But Simon, darling, I thought you said English. I did tell you to check your bag before you got in the car. I had to cancel an appointment to get this to you . . .'

Simon regarded his mother with an expression of utter

contempt and said, 'You are just bloody hopeless. Just rack off!' Then he turned and walked away.

Up until this point she had not even noticed that I was standing there, but now she realised that this rather unpleasant exchange had transpired in front of an audience of one – me. I don't know if she knew who I was, but as an adolescent psychologist I had been invited many times to speak at the school. She looked mortified and said to me apologetically, 'He's been under a lot of stress lately.' She then scurried back to her car and drove off.

Now I don't actually care how much stress Little Lord Fauntleroy had been under. I can think of no circumstance under which it would be acceptable to speak to any human being like that, let alone one's loving mother. In my work as a psychologist I spend a great deal of my time watching parents and their sons and I firmly believe that what I witnessed that day outside the school is on the rise. Can I prove it? I can tell you that in my trips all over Australia, New Zealand and Asia, teachers have told me that this behaviour is increasingly common. Do I have the results of a double-blind, randomised, controlled trial of thousands of families? No. But as someone who works extensively with young people and their families, and is privileged to be invited to schools across Australia, I can tell you that this is real.

When I wrote *The Princess Bitchface Syndrome* in 2006, this type of disrespectful, contemptuous, ungracious behaviour seemed more common among a small sub-section of teenage girls that I worked with. But by the time I wrote its new edition in 2016, this behaviour now seemed to have spilled over to boys. And while they are not as verbal or vitriolic as their sisters, they are physically stronger and can be terrifying in their anger, especially when it is directed towards their mothers, as it so often is.

The trouble with boys like Simon is that they have been brought up to see the world as one giant, personalised, all-singing, all-dancing, 24/7 catering service – exclusively for them. Simon's behaviour is not surprising given that his boorishness has probably been tolerated throughout his childhood, along with the fact that he has likely never been challenged when he refuses to take out the rubbish bins, pick up the dog poo or stack the dishwasher.

Too many of today's parents exhaust themselves trying to make their sons' lives easy by doing things that he can do for himself, leaping in to fix his problems, handing him every single opportunity on a plate, and being his full-time cheerleader. All of these are the ingredients required for a self-absorbed 'boofhead', as one parent told me.

I believe that the child-centred parenting movement, while an understandable response to the cruel, authoritarian parenting practices of the past, has swung too far in the opposite direction. We have become too terrified to say no, to set limits and enforce consequences in case we 'damage' our child's self-esteem. We seem to have turned away from the focus of raising civilised, polite, well-mannered boys and instead have gone to worship at the altar of 'happiness'. We are oblivious to the fact that by not allowing our sons to learn from their own stuff-ups and develop resilience and self-respect, we are creating rudderless, disconnected, bitter and resentful boys who feel they can treat their parents (and other authority figures) in precisely the way Simon treated his mother.

I have written this book to explain how Prince Boofhead Syndrome arises, how you can prevent your son from developing it, and how to cope if you already have a fully functioning Boofhead in your life. The trick is to not buy into the current parenting paradigms of bubble wrap, buddy or helicopter parenting (whichever term you like best), to stop indulging their every whim, and to present a united parenting front. Above all, we have to allow these boys to experience adversity. As the late Mary Tyler Moore once said, 'You can't be brave if you've only had wonderful things happen to you.'

I have enlisted an old friend, Elly Robinson, who is a wonderful writer and researcher to help write this book, but for clarity we've kept it in my voice. My hope is that by the time you have finished reading it, you will know how to parent with authority: how to set non-negotiable rules and enforce them, how to respond when your son whines, demands, complains or yells in order to get his own way, and how to recognise when his behaviour is a sign of more serious issues.

The time has arrived for the self-esteem movement to be relegated to the wastepaper bin of parenting history. The alternative is an intelligent, authoritative parenting style with a developmental perspective. If this appeals to you, read on . . .

Part 1

Understanding Prince Boofhead

In Part 1 I want to outline how a teenage Boofhead can emerge from a home where the parents are loving, nurturing and considerate. A teenage boy is first and foremost a product of his genetic make-up: every brain cell contains twenty-three chromosomes from his mum and twenty-three from his dad, each of which in turn contain hundreds of genes that determine traits such as intelligence, personality and temperament. But we also now know that the environment in which he is raised plays a significant role in how he relates to the world: whether he is curious, resilient and kind, or suspicious, withdrawn and thoughtless. Part 1 illustrates how Boofhead's environment, particularly the parenting that he has received, can influence the final outcome.

Chapter 1
Meet Oliver

Bronwyn is feeling the pressure. Her son, Oliver, is turning 16 next month and has demanded that she organise a fully catered party at the local bowls club. Apparently, he has already sent out invitations on social media. He is also expecting his parents to organise an overseas trip for himself and a couple of friends, which is the usual rite of passage at the exclusive private school he attends.

Bronwyn's husband, Keith, is away on business in South America. Apparently things are not going well and Keith is extremely stressed – if this deal collapses, the company faces financial ruin. Once again Bronwyn has been left to manage the situation at home on her own. It isn't easy, given that she works full time as a lawyer and also has a younger son, James.

She tries for several days to contact the bowls club to see if they can host Oliver's party – which is very stressful given her work commitments. In between, she anxiously examines options for catering. All Oliver will tell her is that 'at least' eighty people will be there, but she has no idea who they are, what sort of food they like, let alone if any have food allergies. She is also concerned about his demand to have a supply of alcohol. She knows that other parents have bought alcohol for their teenagers' parties, but she is worried. As a lawyer she is fully aware that it is an offence to supply alcohol to teenagers without parental permission. This apparently never seems to concern any of the other parents – Oliver often comes home from these parties under the weather and reeking of beer.

After finally getting through to the bowls club, she is devastated to find that the evening Oliver has chosen is already booked. The only option is a Saturday two weeks after his preferred date. She tries the golf club, but to no avail.

When she finally summons up the courage to tell Oliver, he immediately flies into a rage. 'What sort of a stupid cow would leave it this late? You are completely useless. Everyone else's parents manage to book EXACTLY what their sons want,' he screams at her, before storming out of the house.

Bronwyn is not at all surprised by his response. This is how Oliver always behaves when things don't go his way. Unsure of what to do, she books the bowls club, paying the substantial deposit by credit card in case they miss out. She reasons that Oliver can simply tell his friends the party is still on, but just two weeks later. And that she can always cancel if needed, though she has no idea if the deposit will be refunded.

Bronwyn is beginning to feel inadequate again, and hasn't even broached the subject of not being able to book an overseas trip for Oliver this year due to the company's financial problems. It makes her feel physically ill to even think about it.

Lately, she has begun to feel uncomfortable about being alone with Oliver, who seems to revel in using his increasing physical size to intimidate her. Last week, when his brother was out, Oliver thought it was hilarious to pretend to headbutt her each time she tried to talk to him. When she asked him to stop, he laughed in her face and told her to 'loosen up'.

Bronwyn's experience is unpleasant, but is it unusual? Psychologists in clinical practice across the Western world increasingly see evidence of similarly unacceptable behaviour from teen tyrants like Oliver, and these boys do not need to be raised in the leafy suburbs or attend private schools. This behaviour can develop in any family environment where boundaries are nonexistent, creating young men who appear to care only about themselves and readily blame everyone else when things don't go their way. I have decided to call this set of behaviours the Prince Boofhead Syndrome. In psychology, a syndrome is a collection of symptoms that form a condition with a known outcome that requires a special response.

Importantly, the Prince Boofhead Syndrome does not affect all young men who have similar good fortune to Oliver. In fact, through a mixture of personality, temperament and good parenting, it is clear that the vast majority of boys turn out to be fine, considerate, contributing and valuable members of society – even if they experience a period of fairly challenging behaviour. But there is arguably a growing trend where families have a variation on the voracious, spoilt, perpetual adolescent like Oliver. The Prince Boofhead Syndrome is becoming more common and is no longer bound by socio-economic status.

Many parents understandably want their children to have better lives than their own. But what many good parents seem oblivious to is that by creating a world of 'endless fun' where their children are never bored, they are actually doing them a disservice. By buying them so much 'stuff' – potentially enough for three families – and steadfastly ferrying them around from swimming to tennis, karate to Kumon (without a word of thanks in return), their children are given an unrealistic sense of entitlement, aka WRAM – the 'World Revolves Around Me'. The aftermath is an inability for these children to accept responsibility for their actions. In return, their parents, desperate to avoid conflict and confrontation, are likely to respond with even greater indulgence.

Am I making this up? Is this an exaggeration? Another example of a so-called 'expert' engaging in parent bashing? I think not. Despite the warnings of a phalanx of child development experts all over the world, public demonstrations of the Prince Boofhead Syndrome are endless. One of the most extreme examples, in my view, is Texas teenager Ethan Couch. Newspapers reported that in June 2013, at the tender age of 16, Couch was seen on surveillance video stealing two cases of beer from a Walmart store and driving with seven passengers in his father's pickup truck. On the same day as the theft, Couch, who was drunk, illegally driving on a restricted licence and speeding, lost control of the car and hit four people on the side of the road, killing them instantly. Two passengers in Ethan's car were severely injured, with a total of nine people injured or killed in the accident.

A psychologist hired by Couch's defence team claimed that Ethan had 'affluenza' and needed rehabilitation instead of prison; that Ethan was so wealthy and spoilt that he could not tell right from wrong. This is despite the fact that 'affluenza' is not a recognised mental condition in the DSM-V, the American Psychiatric Association's classification and diagnostic tool. Instead, it is a term used by critics of consumerism, such as de Graaf, Wann and Naylor in their book *Affluenza: How Over-consumption is Killing Us – And How to Fight Back*. In this book, affluenza is described as 'a painful, contagious, socially transmitted condition of overload, debt, anxiety, and waste resulting from the dogged pursuit of more'.

The psychologist claimed that the way Couch had been parented 'strongly enabled' the deadly accident, despite the fact that Couch's blood alcohol level was three times the legal limit. While the prosecution argued for twenty years imprisonment, the judge, incredibly, instead sentenced Couch to ten years of drug- and alcohol-free probation for 'intoxication manslaughter', including time in rehabilitation.

But it didn't end there. Three years later, a video emerged on social media showing Couch acting in a manner that was likely to be in violation of his probation deal. Couch fled to Mexico with his mother, Tonya. A two-week manhunt resulted in his capture and deportation to the US, where he was sentenced to nearly two years in prison. His mother faced a ten-year sentence.

The court was told that Couch was parented without reasonable boundaries, and that he was taught 'to an extent' that other people were beneath him and less worthy than him. A witness for the defence claimed that the teenager was a product of 'profoundly dysfunctional parents' who never taught him the consequences of his actions. And, in fact, each of his parents had had their own brushes with the law. His father, Fred, escaped charges related to criminal 'mischief', theft by cheque, impersonating a police officer and assault. Tonya was fined and given a community supervision order for reckless driving in 2013. As they say, the apple never falls very far from the tree.

Thankfully, extreme cases such as this are rare. But it's a good example of how giving a child everything and having zero consequences can go disastrously wrong. So, this book is both a warning and a clarion call to the parents of the Western world. It's time to overthrow the Republic of Weak-Willed Parenting and reinstate wise, firm, fair, present, emotionally engaged and prudent governance.

Let's take a look at what happens in the early and middle years of childhood so we can begin to understand how to avoid placing boys on the pathway to Prince Boofhead-land.

Chapter 2

The early years matter

While a crash course in early childhood development is beyond the scope of this book, some basics may help parents understand that what happens in our early years is mercilessly reflected back to us in the later years. In essence, you reap what you sow.

INFANCY AND EARLY CHILDHOOD

A baby will regularly gurgle and coo to attract the attention of his main caregiver. While this is usually the mother, it can also be the father, grandparent or whom-ever is the baby's significant, constant source of care and attention. These regular interactions, called 'joint atten-tion' sequences, constitute an everyday routine by which a baby and his main caregiver 'check in' with each other. Your baby needs to know that you are nearby, as it helps him to feel safe and secure, thus building the foundations for later social and emotional development.

This safety and security means that your son, as a newly mobile toddler, can explore his world confidently and enthusiastically, helped along by you squealing with delight every time he inserts the last piece of his Ravensburger five-piece jigsaw puzzle in the right spot.

Like most youngsters, he is naturally resilient. He will patiently build towers out of blocks, watch them fall down with delight and then rebuild them in a different way. He will try to climb a tree or a piece of furniture, slip and fall and cheerfully try a different method to get up. During this period he needs to know that you are nearby, but if you are hovering over him with a look of fear or anxiety, constantly telling him, 'Be careful', 'Don't fall', 'Don't make a mess' or, worse, 'Here, let me do it for you', it teaches him that the world is a dangerous place, that he is incompetent and that to fail is bad.

If he is allowed to explore his environment and is given the opportunity to experiment and make mistakes, his brain becomes switched on to learning, which, unsurprisingly, is a great precursor to school engagement. Children are wired to learn through free play, not structured activities arranged and controlled by adults, or by the ubiquitous electronic babysitter of the modern era – the iPad. Nothing lights up the child's brain like three-dimensional play with a caring adult.

If his parents understand that he is not neurologically equipped to make major decisions or self-regulate his behaviour and emotions, they will clearly point out what is expected behaviour ('It is not okay to take the toy away from your friend') and use distraction ('Come over here and we'll find another toy to play with on these shelves').

If, as he gets older, his parents continue to provide clear

rules about what is acceptable behaviour and what is not, and enforce them reliably and fairly, he will enter school knowing that the world doesn't revolve around him. For example, every time he hits his baby sister, he is sent to his room; if he interrupts a parent who is speaking on the phone or to another adult, he is politely told to wait until they are finished; if he plays with his toys together with a visiting friend, he is told how great he is at sharing.

THE MIDDLE YEARS

Until recently, the middle primary school years (grades 3–6) were regarded as a relatively uneventful 'lull' between the chaos of early childhood and the intensity of adolescence. This is where children are honing the astonishing range of skills they've learned in the last seven or so years, including reading, writing, swimming, riding a bike, understanding that other people have different points of view, and countless other abilities. Increasingly, however, we've heard stories of 8-year-old boys having body image issues and 10-year-old boys having emotional meltdowns at the drop of a hat. So what is going on?

We've always known that boys have a testosterone surge at around the age of eight or nine (an early stage of puberty called adrenarche), but recent studies from the Murdoch Children's Research Institute indicate that this may be a more important stage of development than previously thought. In particular, boys who enter this stage earlier than their peers show different brain patterns, and their parents report a higher incidence of behavioural problems. Other changes include greasy skin and strong body odour. Science journalist Vivienne Parry suggests that this is why a raucous party of twenty 7-year-old boys smells a whole lot different than it did when they were five years old.

It's not clear at this stage why boys appear to be more sensitive to these changes than girls (who go through a similar hormonal surge in the middle years). According to Professor George Patton, despite there being no obvious external signs associated with adrenarche, there is in fact a great deal going on for boys. The implication, he believes, is that we should no longer think of middle childhood as a 'quiet period' of development. Many parents think of these later primary school years as the laid-back, calm-before-the-teenage-storm years, and tend to take it easy when it comes to enforcing rules and setting boundaries. But with new influences such as marketing and social media, parents need to think far more proactively about how to create effective educational, social and emotional environments that promote healthy development during these years. I talk about these in Part 2.

DO WE RAISE BOYS DIFFERENTLY?

Whether we like it or not, research shows that there are clear differences in the way many parents and other adults behave around children depending on whether they are male or female. Girls are seen as delicate, soft creatures and treated accordingly, while boys are handled more roughly, to the point where the number of head injuries in boys in the first three months of life is higher than in girls, primarily due to how frequently they are dropped.

There is no doubt, in addition to this picture, that toys are marketed to gender – princess dolls and pink dollhouses for the girls; trucks and superheroes for the boys. In the long term, this may contribute to certain unhealthy behaviours, such as girls focusing on their physical appearance, and boys on physical exertion that often models aggressive or violent attitudes and behaviours. Cultural expectations further shape gender-biased parenting. Boys, for example, are encouraged to be competitive and take chances, while girls are encouraged to be cooperative and nurturing. In reality, we need to help children develop a mix of all of these competencies to become well-adjusted, happy adults.

THE IMPORTANCE OF DADS

Children have different relationships with their fathers than they do with their mothers, and this independent relationship is an important one. Fathers are more likely to engage in 'roughhousing' physical play that is exciting and unpredictable, and they are also more likely to encourage children to take risks and embrace challenges. Right from birth, Dad (or the important male figure in a child's life) represents the 'who, what and how' of manhood. And there is a great deal of research about the significance of having a trusted male influence in the lives of both young men and young women. Fathers play a critical role in child development, including the support of academic performance and social, emotional and psychological adjustment. For example, fathers' parenting has been associated with the quality of intimate relationships reported by young adults. Also, boys who have strong relationships with their fathers are less likely to engage in delinquent behaviours, and strong father–son relationships are associated with fewer depressive symptoms in boys.

The truth is, however, that many fathers who work full time spend very little time with their children, especially if time at home is taken up with household chores such as paying bills and home maintenance. The justification is that they are providing for their family – by working to pay for a nice house and perhaps the fees for a so-called 'good' school – but this lack of fathering may not be in the child's best interests. Dads who feel guilty about not spending more time with their sons may also be reluctant to insist on good behaviour, to establish rules and routines and to implement consequences when rules are broken.

The less practice fathers have at being involved, the less confident they feel about taking on a more active parenting role, which means they're even less likely to try. In such cases, mothers may feel compelled to take the disciplinary reins, which can be challenging for family stability, especially if the mother feels resentful towards the father because of his lack of involvement. In addition, the superglue strength of the mother–child bond may mean some mums can struggle to balance their urge to keep their son safe with the son's need to develop independence.

The father–son relationship may become even more difficult to maintain in the case of separation or divorce. According to research conducted by the Australian

Bureau of Statistics in 2013, 500 000 children aged 0–17 years had one biological parent living elsewhere. Of these, almost half saw this parent at least once per fortnight, but a quarter saw the other parent less than once per year, or never. Older children in particular were less likely to have contact with the non-resident parent: only 35 per cent of children aged 15–17 saw the other parent at least once a fortnight. The non-resident parent was five times more likely to be the father than the mother (16 per cent of all families with children aged 0–17 years were headed by single mothers, while only 3 per cent were headed by single fathers).

In his book *Fatherless America*, David Blankenhorn calls the notable numbers of fathers who are missing in their children's lives 'the most destructive trend of our generation'. For those children who do see their father on occasion, the impact of bucketloads of parental guilt (for both parties) means many parents seek to make it up to children by indulging them and becoming hesitant to set limits and boundaries. The 'popularity contest' that some separated parents engage in can leave their offspring with no moral compass. Instead, their indulgent or laissez-faire parenting meets a child's physical needs, but provides little love, guidance and wisdom.

We know that young men and women experience relationships and emotions with great intensity, and broken hearts and busted friendships are a very real experience. Yet when it comes to the big discussions about love, healthy relationships or building positive professional reputations, dads are often nowhere to be seen.

Teenage boys in particular can find it very difficult to talk to either parent about friends, school and how they are feeling. When boys don't talk, it is often a way of protecting and preserving themselves. It should not be seen as disinterest or a lack of need for emotional closeness. In some instances, this monosyllabic or silent treatment emerges from childhood where, somewhere along the way, they have internalised the message that parental love and approval is contingent upon good behaviour and achievement. So when they inevitably make a mistake or fail at something, they are so afraid of rejection and censure that they shut down.

For some fathers, the easiest way to get more involved is to start with a mutual interest – say, a sporting or musical activity – and to be responsible for taking children to the practice sessions, games and performances. (Of course the interest doesn't have to be mutual, but it makes conversation easier.) It is also important for mothers to step aside and allow their partners to take on this responsibility. Fathers need to demonstrate respect and compassion for others, especially respect for women and girls. There is also a great role for uncles, grandfathers and male family friends, all of whom can contribute to the psychological template of what it means to be male.

THE IMPORTANCE OF DELAYED GRATIFICATION

Many of the Prince Boofheads I meet are not only showered in material goods but also receive said goods the moment they express a desire for them. This has the effect of teaching children that they can expect the best of everything without expending any effort – also known as a sense of entitlement. Being able to wait for what you want is the ability to delay gratification, and research has shown that a deficit in this area is related to poor outcomes in adulthood.

One of the best-known studies to measure delayed gratification in children was the marshmallow experiment, conducted in the 1960s at Stanford University by Professor Walter Mischel. In the original study, pre-school-aged children sat with a marshmallow in front of them for 15 minutes while the researcher left the room. The children were told that if they waited until the researcher returned before eating the marshmallow, they would be rewarded with a second marshmallow. In a series of follow-up studies, Mischel found that children who waited for the second marshmallow (i.e. demonstrated delayed gratification) generally had better outcomes later in life, including higher university entry scores, less likelihood of substance abuse, and lower body mass indexes. Teaching children that they can tolerate a delay before a desire is fulfilled has long-reaching consequences for their adult success.

In 2013, Celeste Kidd and colleagues from the University of Rochester reproduced Mischel's experiment, but with a twist. Prior to the marshmallow test, the experimenters were shown to be *reliable* or *unreliable* based on whether they delivered the goods in a different activity. The children were then randomly assigned to either of these experimenters in the marshmallow test.

The children with a *reliable* experimenter waited on average four times longer to eat the marshmallow than those with an *unreliable* experimenter. This suggests that children who trust their parents to stick to their guns are more able to wait for a reward.

So how do we help children learn to delay gratification? One way is to encourage children to identify the difference between their needs and wants. Psychologists routinely suggest the following strategies to help with this.

'I have another idea'

When children are very young and still developing their cognitive skills, asking them to think of an alternative to what they 'need' works brilliantly. For example, 'No, we don't need ice cream for lunch. What else could we have that's healthy and yummy?'

As they get older and are able to think in a more sophisticated way, the technique is to get them to consider different options and the consequences of making a particular choice. This is known as critical thinking – the ability to objectively analyse a situation and evaluate the options to solve a problem or make the best decision. It is a skill that develops slowly from around the age of seven, if parents allow children opportunities for practice.

For example, 'If we buy this now, what will happen when you want something new on your birthday and the money has been spent?' Asking children questions and allowing them to come to their own conclusions about what they need versus what they want is a more sensible and strategic ploy than just saying 'No' all the time.

'I'd like one, but I can wait'

Psychologists have discovered that children notice, process and mimic the actions and behaviour of the adults in their lives from a very early age. This can be a source of much hilarity for everyone in the extended family, but there is also a serious side. If you throw a wobbly when you make a mistake, your children will learn to do this, too. If you use the f-word in the presence of your children, don't be surprised if they start swearing like a trooper.

The same goes for learning about wants versus needs. If a child hears the adults in his life regularly say, 'I need a new [insert gadget]', this will be the message he sucks up like a vacuum cleaner and regurgitates.

The solution is to rephrase your own 'I need that' statements to 'I'd really like that, but I don't *need* it.' By reducing your own need for instant gratification, you can transmit useful messages to your son that might prevent later problems.

Encourage philanthropy

The act of giving creates solid connections between people and helps to build a happier society for everyone. If there are opportunities to get your son involved in your own or the school's philanthropic activities, it will help him to recognise that he already *has* everything he needs. As we saw in chapter 1, the rampant 'affluenza' that many of our children are surrounded with from birth actually ends up being a major risk factor in the development of the Prince Boofhead Syndrome.

When boys reach out to others in need, it encourages

them to feel gratitude for what they do have. Early exposure is crucial, with research demonstrating that boys learn to be generous by having the experience of offering to help someone else or making a donation and processing how it feels. You don't have to coerce them into regularly performing one charitable act a day. When they are young, you can offer them a smorgasbord of altruistic ideas and let them choose one they like. As they grow older, hopefully they will develop their own ideas.

For example, you could add a small amount to your son's pocket money in primary school, but specify that it must go towards charity. Collect the coins each pocket money 'pay day' and when there are enough, go to a site such as Kiva.org and support social entrepreneurs all over the world.

Encourage financial literacy

Another way to teach children the difference between wants and needs is to give them an allowance (or pocket money) that they must use for some of life's essentials, such as mobile phone credit. This works especially well with teenagers. Put them in charge of their money and they'll quickly work out that they can't text their friends when the money is gone. Remember, though, that this requires you to be able to resist the temptation to respond to their many requests for a top up – or else the lesson is lost.

Chapter 3

The adolescent years

Adolescence is a period of rapid development across a number of domains – physical, cognitive, social and emotional – all of which occur against a backdrop of complex socio-cultural influences, including family, school, community and technology. It's an incredibly important and generally misunderstood time of life. That's why adding a developmental perspective to your parenting arsenal is one of the most useful and helpful things you can do for yourself and your sons. It will help you understand why they don't automatically do what you tell them to any more, and why they roll their eyes so dramatically that you worry they'll detach a retina.

Psychologist Steve Biddulph is well known for his considerable expertise on child development. In a 2010 interview with *The Telegraph*, he deftly describes a child's journey into early adolescence as recycling 'their baby-hood' due to physical changes in the brain. They need parents to provide structure as they are unable to organise themselves and make decisions. Biddulph advises parents to try to keep their sense of humour and not to give up.

PHYSICAL DEVELOPMENT

Pubertal timing in boys is generally less well understood than in girls, for whom there has been a documented decrease in the age of onset of puberty over recent decades. The lack of research on puberty in boys is mainly because the age of menarche (first period) in girls is easier to measure than the onset of puberty in boys. (What teenage boy wants a physical examination of his testicular volume, or to disclose the timing of his first ejaculation?) One interesting insight, however, comes from the collection of data by boys' choirs on voice-breaking. Voice-breaking, while commonly occurring later than other signs of puberty, is a more readily noted indicator of puberty. Records from the Leipzig choir showed that for male singers in the mid-1700s, the median age for voice-breaking was 18 years. In contrast, boys in the Copenhagen Municipal Choir School between 1994 and 2003 experienced voice-breaking at a median age of 10.4 years.

We know far more about outcomes for boys who go through puberty earlier or later than their friends. Data from the Longitudinal Study of Australian Children indicates that around 6 per cent of boys have begun puberty by age eight or nine. Boys who develop early may physically look like adults, enjoy athletic advantages and experience higher levels of self-esteem, but there may be a darker side to early puberty for them. The same longitudinal research showed that these boys were more likely to have greater behavioural, emotional and social difficulties. These include greater levels of mental health problems such as depression and substance abuse, but also behaviours such as vandalism, property damage, shoplifting and truancy. Girls also had difficulties, but the increased behavioural problems only occurred in boys. On the flipside, late maturing boys were more likely to report greater feelings of inadequacy, social rejection and inferiority.

Both early and late maturing young men are likely to need our support and understanding more than others. Those who mature early are cognitively and emotionally still children, but grappling with new stressors that they are often not ready for. For example, they may be expected to compete in high-level sporting and athletic competitions (given their developmental advantage) without the necessary cognitive or social skills. Daily media feeds regularly feature stories of young sportsmen who are navigating these challenges. Early maturing boys may also be confused by their emerging sexual desires and urges to experiment with extreme risk-taking behaviour. Supportive parenting is a known protective factor for early maturing boys, whereas harsh and unpredictable parenting increases the likelihood of poor outcomes. We need to respond to teenage boys in an age-appropriate way – especially when the rest of the world is reacting to their body size rather than their brain development.

Research suggests that late bloomers, on the other hand, tend to have lower self-esteem than their same-age peers, and a higher incidence of depressed moods and poor body image. However, late maturation tends to be less associated with negative emotions and behavioural problems compared to earlier maturation, and some studies suggest that late maturing boys are more responsible, sociable and cooperative.

COGNITIVE DEVELOPMENT

When a bearded, 188-centimetre 16-year-old is standing in front of you in a rage, it's easy to forget that his mental cutlery is very different to yours. As I like to say, the adolescent brain is all accelerator and no brake. The accelerator is the limbic system – the area of the brain that influences emotions, motivation, mood and sensations of pain and pleasure. Brain research shows that the limbic system in adolescents is hypersensitive to the rewarding buzz they get from risk-taking. Yet, at the same time, the prefrontal cortex – the 'brake' part of our brains that regulates emotions, makes complex decisions and understands future consequences – is still under construction. In fact, the prefrontal cortex won't be fully functional until the early to mid-twenties. Adolescents are also still learning to recognise emotions in others, which goes some way towards explaining the frustrating patterns of self-interest and self-centredness at this age.

The teen brain is very malleable, which means we should be especially careful about the types of experiences that teenagers are exposed to. According to psychologist Dr Laurence Steinberg, the adolescent brain is more vulnerable to chemical and hormonal damage from drugs and stress, but it is also more receptive to learning new skills and absorbing new information. Therefore, brain development is maximised by providing a rich array of positive activities that push your child beyond their level of comfort (but not so far that success is unachievable), and setting boundaries that limit their exposure to negative influences (see Part 2).

SOCIAL AND EMOTIONAL DEVELOPMENT

Aside from dealing with the intense physical changes taking place in their bodies and brains, teenage boys are also beginning to tackle the important developmental tasks of adolescence: achieving independence from parents and other adults; developing positive peer and intimate relationships; forming a realistic, stable identity (including gender and body image); and acquiring the skills for future economic independence. In pre-industrial societies, the transition to many of these adult roles occurred around four years after puberty for boys (two for girls). In today's society, longer periods of education, plus delayed marriage and childrearing often mean that adolescence continues for a decade and beyond. This means that parents often have involvement in their sons' development for far longer than in previous generations, which has both positive and negative aspects, as we shall see.

During adolescence, all parents become a source of intense and unbridled embarrassment to their offspring. When you drop your son at a party you may well be asked to park a few houses away, and there is definitely no yelling 'Daddy loves you!' out the window as you drive away. Yet, despite this temporary period of parenting obsolescence, you need to be your son's greatest supporter whether he appreciates it or not. Young men actually crave closeness, comfort, unconditional acceptance and the security that comes with a routine environment, even though they would rather walk over hot coals than admit this. But they also need structure and firm boundaries that not only contribute to a sense of security, but give them a starting point for developing their own moral compasses. Parenting with intelligence and a loving but firm hand during this critical phase of early and middle adolescence is essential if you are going to avoid the syndrome described in this book.

Emancipating from parents

The task of emancipating from parents and other adult caregivers or relatives in early and middle adolescence has historically been seen as a 'separation'. These days, it is better understood as young people and their parents negotiating a new relationship that balances the young person's need for autonomy and independence with the parents' need to know their child is safe. The process will be different for each child, as adults must take into account the individual differences that stem from the young person's personality, temperament and emotional maturity.

Indeed, a growing number of young adults continue to live with their parents or return home after a period away. (The silver lining is that those who leave home later often have more regular contact and provide more help to their parents even after they eventually leave.) Combined with later ages for marriage and children, the timelines for adolescence and young adulthood just keep extending. But as Dr Laurence Steinberg points out, delayed adulthood (defined by a stable relationship, children and/or financial independence) is not necessarily a bad thing – it all depends on how the time is spent. A young person who is studying, for example, is stimulating higher order cognitive abilities and self-control in ways that just getting older will not.

A parent's role in the teenage years is to provide structure and monitoring; to know where their sons are, who they are with and what they are doing; and to be in the background keeping things running as usual. This is not about whether or not you trust your son, but about understanding that his capacity to assess danger is underdeveloped at this age, and that he needs help to make good decisions and to learn to predict the consequences of his actions. His brain is more wired to reward than risk assessment.

Making friends

As boys grow older there is often a change from forming relationships based largely on shared interests (e.g. art, music, video games or sport) to those based on sharing ideas and feelings, mutual trust, and understanding each other.

The ability to obtain, maintain and retain good friend-ships is one of the most significant predictors of wellbeing later in life. In other words, the peer relationships formed at this time can play a powerful role in providing support and connection as the young person navigates the path to adulthood. But these relationships may also encourage unhealthy risk-taking behaviour such as drug and alcohol abuse, unsafe sexual practices, truancy and antisocial behaviour such as theft and vandalism. This is why it is so important for you to keep the lines of communication open. Adolescent boys (and Prince Boofheads in particular) are hair-trigger sensitive to control, so stay interested and engaged without being judgemental or anxious.

Parents' ability to help their sons make good choices about friendships diminishes over time, so it is crucial to get in early – get to know who they are hanging out with, welcome them into your home and let them raid the pantry. Be a taxi driver and get to know the families of your son's friends. You can have a greater influence in steering a path towards good choices than you think. But of course, this only works if you have a strong connection with your son, and connection requires communication. (I talk more about communication on page 71.)

Forming an identity

Figuring out the answer to the question 'Who am I?' is arguably a lifelong process, though a lot of the heavy lifting takes place in adolescence. Teenagers may become obsessed with their appearance and whether or not they are 'normal'. They may begin to question the values of their parents and the wider culture, to experiment with different countercultures and to explore questions of race, gender and sexuality. Privacy is paramount, and they demand the freedom to make some of their own decisions, even if they are not yet adept at understanding the consequences.

Engaging with school or work

Ask boys in Year 7 what they like most about school, and their responses will often be limited to 'sport', 'lunchtime' or 'the home bell' (if they answer at all). As they mature, they are expected to appreciate that education is an important step on the path to economic independence. Indeed, research from the Australian Institute of Health and Welfare shows that completing Year 12 improves transitions to further study and employment. Yet research from the Mitchell Institute at Victoria University has found that close to 1 in 4 Australian students do not finish Year 12, and that dropout rates are highest in remote and economically disadvantaged areas. In addition, the 2015 Mission Australia Youth Survey found that almost three times the number of young men compared to young women indicated that they did not intend to complete Year 12.

While we know that boys are more likely than girls to be disengaged with school, we are not sure why this happens. Some researchers suggest that it has to do with societal expectations that 'boys will be boys', and that our widespread tolerance of their more disruptive and defiant behaviour sends a signal that disengagement is what is expected of them. Others say that it has more to do with the way that we tend to structure our learning environments as 'one size fits all' sausage factories, expecting boys and girls to conform to the same expectations when there are actually enormous differences in the way they learn.

We also know that one of the important predictors of academic success in boys is the relationship that they have with their teachers. Having at least one teacher with a sense of humour and an understanding of what boys need can inspire a love of learning, which is arguably the whole point of our children attending school.

At this stage of their sons' lives, parents need to have their finger on the academic pulse so that they can be alert to any problems early on. This includes the possibility that their sons may have an undiagnosed anxiety disorder or learning disability. Parents need to be enthusiastic about both the academic side of school and extracurricular activities. If parents take an interest, then the likelihood is that their sons will follow.

When Simon's humanities teacher handed out the latest assignment, he and his classmates groaned audibly. Over the term, the students were required to record waste disposal in their home and calculate a number of different measures that showed the household's recycling habits, before writing it up in a 1500-word report. Simon had no intention of completing this report – what was the point? Not surprisingly, when reports came out at the end of the year, Simon had not completed any of the work and had failed humanities. When his mother queried the mark, Simon told her how stupid the assignment was, how none of his friends had done it either and really, what did the teacher expect? His mother agreed that the expectation seemed unreasonable, and let the matter drop. After all, she knew Simon was very clever and didn't really need humanities for a career of any importance.

This is a clear case of a parent who has not kept their finger on the academic pulse. Not knowing what was going on in her son's schooling may have been an excuse in the 1980s, but in this age of online monitoring, schools keep parents in the loop about truancy, punctuality and assessment. Log in daily to your school's portal and see what subjects he has today and what assignments are due. This is not helicopter parenting, but part of parenting a son, as is the clear expectation that no matter what the subject or who is teaching it, your son engages in the subject and performs to the best of his ability.

Boys live in the moment, especially during the early years of puberty. The bottom line is that Prince Boofhead Syndrome occurs when parents give their sons an abundance of cash but not enough of their time.

Chapter 4
The emergence of Prince Boofhead

In the last chapter I talked briefly about the physiological, social and emotional changes that occur in adolescence. While it can be a stressful period, the majority of teenage boys emerge as capable, considerate young men. For some teens and their families, however, the journey can be very rough, and not for the reasons you might think. Every week I see angry, belligerent young men with problems at school, at work and in their relationships. Yet these boys have not been raised in families scarred by substance abuse or crime. They've been raised by loving, intelligent parents who are trying their best.

It makes sense that parents want their children to be happy. It is often echoed in sentiments such as 'a parent is only as happy as their unhappiest child.' But what happens when you systematically try to protect your children from the inevitable challenges and disappointments that life serves up? What happens when children are constantly buffered from the possibility that they have contributed to a less than ideal outcome, reinforcing the false belief that they are flawless?

Increasingly, our children are rewarded for the smallest and most insignificant of actions. If you check many of the games they are playing on their latest device, it's not difficult to find one that congratulates them on simply setting up the account, let alone the coins and jewels they receive for winning their first 15-second battle. Parents contribute to this never-ending praise by telling them 'good job' for every painting brought home from kindergarten and every mouthful of yoghurt they manage to spoon into their own mouths.

The problem is that this type of parenting is instilling in children the dangerous belief that they are *more likely* to succeed than their peers, and that they are destined for greatness. This in turn sets up a scaffold of expectations; that is, if the child doesn't outperform those around him, then there is something wrong with him. As they move through the developmental stages, including involvement in school, sports and other pursuits, an overdeveloped sense of responsibility to be perfect sits alongside a profoundly underdeveloped set of skills for coping when the inevitable failures or mistakes occur. That is, when they fall short of the unattainable mark. These kids are behavioural and emotional time bombs.

PRINCE BOOFHEAD AND THE DEVELOPMENTAL TASKS OF ADOLESCENCE

So how does this lack of resilience affect Prince Boofhead as he negotiates the developmental tasks of adolescence, including emancipating from parents, making friends, forming an identity and engaging with school or work?

Resentful dependence on his parents

Prince Boofhead has zero respect for his elders. He is not interested in the thoughts or opinions of his parents, relatives or even teachers, as he has access to the single most comprehensive (and always accurate!) information source in history – the internet. He is also unlikely to have a relationship with a mentor, such as a coach, uncle or other adult male, which we know is a protective factor against poor mental health outcomes for young people (see page 48 for more about mentors).

Boofhead may not only demand that his parents fund him during his secondary and higher education, but he will also expect continuing financial support until 'someone' offers him employment that is worthy of his time, intellect, skills or family standing. Boofhead has an unrealistic idea about what he deserves to earn, including a complete lack of intent to start at the bottom of any career ladder and earn a starting salary.

At my clinic, I have had young Boofheads stare at me and state, 'Doc, they gave birth to me, I didn't choose this – it's not my fault I need to study and don't have time to work. I need to have a life, too. It's their obligation as parents.'

Rather than acquiesce to encouragements about getting a part-time job, Prince Boofhead will simply tell his parents that it's far too difficult to get a job these days or that, if he does have to work, it will negatively impact his capacity to study and get good results. How could any parent dare put their child in such a risky position?

Troubled friendships

Prince Boofhead has been led to believe, via consistent messages from his parents (and quite possibly others who have fallen for his rooster ruse), that he is 'special'. He values himself over others to the extent that he disregards their feelings and wishes. His innate belief in his own greatness also provides him with justification for belittling or bullying others, particularly his mother. When it suits him, he behaves in an exploitative manner in order to get what he wants regardless of the impact on anyone else, because 'they don't understand' or 'they don't matter'.

In conjunction with this belief in his own specialness, when Boofhead thinks that someone he respects has overlooked or slighted him (for example, they don't pick him in the basketball team), what often follows is a ballistic emotional and behavioural meltdown. The person who slighted him is likely to be demonised and vilified, relegated to his long personal list of pathetic, useless people.

This constant need for admiration can take a toll, not only on Prince Boofhead but also on those around him, who are left to pick up the pieces when Humpty hits the floor.

Not surprisingly, Prince Boofhead has difficulty developing genuine and trusting relationships with others. At school, when other young people were seeking and building genuine connections, he concentrated on controlling the social environment by being 'the best'. He still sees many of his peers as beneath him and chooses to hold court with other young men who 'will be investment bankers', but secretly believes that he will be better than any of them.

If he hasn't learned to build genuine and authentic connections by his early twenties, it sadly won't become any easier. This is likely to impact his personal relationships, including those that are intimate (see page 162), as well as social and work relationships.

> Connor grew up in a family, school and community that placed a strong emphasis on designer clothes, extravagant cars and expensive houses as a way of showing status and success. His parents gave him everything he wanted to ensure that he never missed out. It's hardly surprising that Connor ended up focusing on material goods as the way to define happiness. He was not interested in setting goals and achieving them, nor was he interested in connecting with others or trying new experiences. On his 13th birthday, for example, his parents were planning a huge family celebration, but when asked by a neighbour if he was looking forward to it, Connor's reply was nonchalant. 'Nah. Not really.' When the neighbour asked why, Connor replied, 'Birthdays are no big deal. If I want something, I just get it.'

A fragile sense of self

Despite his confident veneer, Prince Boofhead has a very fragile ego. He is often preoccupied with fantasies of wealth, power and success, but has no understanding of the work required to achieve them. Nor is he able to tolerate the idea of making a mistake. Being wrong is simply not a possibility that Boofhead entertains, let alone owning up to what might be considered a personal failing. But when things do go wrong, as they will, take cover. If he is in a situation where things haven't gone his way or turned out as well as he thought, instead of accepting this as a mistake or taking responsibility where appropriate, he is likely to go to great lengths to attribute the cause to someone else, or move the goalposts.

When times are tough, Prince Boofhead will describe feeling lonely and disconnected. This may be okay if he is achieving academically, when he can draw on a temporary sense of self that is 'good'. When he can't draw on anything like this, life can feel pointless. When he expresses this sentiment, his family or partner erupt (again) in a flurry of activity to try to absorb his emotions and compensate for him. But they can't – even though, in his mind, they damn well should, since it's really their fault. They can provide love and support, but ultimately it is up to Prince Boofhead to absorb his own disappointments, learn from them and move forward, having become a better and stronger person for weathering the storm.

Poor school/work engagement

Despite his know-it-all facade, Prince Boofhead has a

crippling fear of failure and is prone to self-sabotage as a result. He may procrastinate, daydream or allow himself to be constantly distracted by peers so that he is unable to concentrate fully on learning tasks. Yet he still expects to do well and, if he does get a poor mark or, worse, is subject to criticism of any kind, he may fall into a rage-filled quicksand of depression.

Some Boofheads may move the goalposts completely, claiming that school or work is a monumental waste of their time and far beneath their dignity. They rush assignments, cut classes and scrape by on the bare minimum.

> Since finishing school two years ago, Scott seemed less and less interested in finding a job and was increasingly aggressive towards his parents if they asked what he planned to do next. Instead, he spent many hours locked in his room playing video games and on chat sites with friends. His father, Bryan, frustrated at paying Scott's way in the world with no recognition or thanks, rang an old friend who owned a number of busy restaurants in the city area to see if he might have a job that would interest Scott. When Bryan mentioned the opportunity to work in the kitchen of a well-known, top-end restaurant for a couple of nights a week, Scott scoffed at him, rolled his eyes and said, 'Whatever pleases you . . .'
>
> On the first night, just as Bryan was about to leave the house to pick him up, Scott walked through the door. Bryan, surprised, asked Scott what happened. Scott replied, 'Chefs are the biggest try-hards in the

world. If the head chef tried to tell me what to do one more time, I was going to punch him, so I told him to get f*cked instead and walked out.'

This is a clear case of Prince Boofhead Syndrome. In the first instance, parents should not be chauffeuring their 20-year-old sons anywhere, unless said offspring are sporting broken limbs. Scott must be responsible for finding himself a job, and the best way to encourage his enthusiasm for joining the real world is for his parents to cut off his cash supply. Bryan needs to stop paying for Scott's internet, phone or other privileges and then gently break it to him that he will also need to pay board to cover living expenses.

All boys will display Boofheadish behaviour from time to time. They'll answer back, give us the stink eye, tell us they hate us or point-blank refuse to do something we ask. This is normal as they tackle the developmental tasks of adolescence. They're testing the limits – asking, 'What can I get away with?' – and in the process they begin to understand how the world works and their place in it. The Prince Boofhead Syndrome arises when parents are unable or unwilling to set boundaries, leaving their sons no choice but to keep pushing until they find some – often those enforced by authorities such as schools or the police.

Viewed from the outside, these young men may appear selfish, reckless or even ruthless, but underneath the bravado is a tissue-thin sense of self. Without boundaries, Prince Boofhead does not learn to deal with the rage and frustration of missing out, or the disappointment of failure. He doesn't learn how to wait his turn, to share, or to see himself as a member of a team or a community. In effect, he becomes a young man who is largely incapable of coping with school, university, relationships, the workplace and society in general.

Part 2

Parenting
Prince Boofhead

In this section I want to talk about what parents can do to encourage children to develop the resilience that Prince Boofheads are so sorely lacking. Indeed, the Australian Psychological Society's 2016 Compass for Life Wellbeing Survey paints a pretty grim picture of young people's resilience. It found that young Australians had significantly lower scores on engagement, positive emotion and overall wellbeing than those aged over 35. And only 45 per cent of those surveyed had a strong sense of belonging to their community. This sense of belonging is key in resilience research and should be hugely worrying to all who work in education and welfare.

Put simply, resilience is the capacity to face, overcome and be strengthened by adversity. The most famous study that looked at resilience was by Emmy Werner and Ruth Smith in Kauai, Hawaii. Werner and Smith followed all of the children born on the island in 1955 through to the age of 45. They found that many children who lived in adverse conditions (characterised by poverty, perinatal stress and disorganised family environments) developed serious learning and/or behavioural problems by the age of 10.

However, there were a group of children in these adverse environments who still had very good outcomes in later years; in fact, more and more of the children began to do better as they got older. The difference for those with better outcomes was that they had access to one or more 'protective factors'. These included:

- social and emotional competencies, such as being able to recognise others' feelings, manage anger, solve problems and resolve conflict
- access to at least one caring and committed adult outside the family who helped them to feel safe, valued and listened to
- the belief that they could determine their own destiny, and that what happened to them was a result of their own actions
- a sense of meaning, purpose and belonging (for some this was related to practising a religion, while for others it was meaningful involvement in a sport, their community or a particular cause); these children recognised that they were a part of something bigger than themselves
- activities or skills they excelled in that preoccupied their days (their 'islands of competence').

This section looks at some of the ways we can help to build these critical protective factors into our children's lives.

Chapter 5

Help him find his 'spark'

Psychologist Robert Brooks first coined the term 'islands of competence' to describe activities or skills that help people feel that they are worthwhile and useful human beings. Research has found that the earlier we discover something we are good at and that we enjoy doing for our own sake rather than to please others, the better our outcomes are later in life. In his book and TED Talk, Peter Benson called it 'finding your spark'.

A spark can be:

- a natural skill or talent, such as playing a musical instrument or sport
- a commitment, such as volunteering or being environmentally conscious
- a characteristic, such as being a good listener.

Sometimes it can take a while for children to find their spark, which is why it is important for parents to encourage children to try different activities. However, this does not mean you need to enrol your 2-year-old in

Japanese lessons. Nor should you expect your 16-year-old to suddenly take up cricket if he has never held a bat. If he is not sure what he wants to try, find out what activities are offered at school, and perhaps what his friends are interested in, and encourage him to take part in something.

Finding his spark is important for building resilience as it not only strengthens his sense of competence and self-mastery but also gives him the opportunity to make new friends and develop stronger ties with the broader community. He may also find a mentor.

For Prince Boofhead, the problem is that he often thinks he is magnificently talented at everything, so does not see the point in focusing his attention on one activity. Of course, the truth is that he is so terrified of failure that he will not allow himself to develop a passion for a particular activity, which can preclude him from developing genuine feelings of competence.

THE POWER OF MENTORS

A mentor is someone who can offer advice, support and encouragement to a young person as they navigate the vicissitudes of life. Commonly mentors are of the same gender, and this is especially valuable for boys who may not spend a lot of time with their fathers. Importantly, a mentor will provide realistic feedback on a mentee's progress – they will not (as some parents are wont to do) tell them that everything they do is brilliant or, worse, that everything they do is shite. Giving praise when it is genuinely earned helps a young man develop a realistic sense of self.

Indigenous societies understand that adolescent boys need guidance and support from the whole community, not just from their parents. Older men teach them a huge range of skills, including fishing, hunting, boat-building and many other crafts. The mentors also pass on cultural traditions and knowledge, and help keep the young men in line.

In our Western society, the apprenticeship system is an invaluable source of mentoring. Young men are assigned to a single experienced tradesperson and, in the process, learn not only the skills necessary for the job but also valuable life lessons. Unfortunately, these days most tradespeople are educated in colleges, so that special one-to-one mentoring relationship can be diluted.

Ask any man if they had a mentor when growing up, and many will be able to name an uncle, a godfather or close family friend who gave them support and acknowledgement in early adulthood. A mentor can also be a coach or teacher who offers advice on life skills (e.g. choosing a career, communicating with family or handling a relationship break-up), but only when asked. This is very different to a father, who by definition, tends to step in and tell his son how to live his life.

UNCONDITIONAL LOVE

Although it is important for young people to find their spark, parents need to be wary of putting pressure on their children to achieve. Start balancing this when he is very young by praising effort as well as achievement. So instead of showering him with accolades (whether deserved or not) with statements such as 'What a clever boy!', 'That's amazing!' or 'Wow! I can see your work hanging in the National Gallery!' you can say:

- 'I can see you worked really hard to finish that.'
- 'I love how you got really stuck into that project.'
- 'It's great how you didn't give up – you kept on trying until you were happy with it.'

Show your son that you love him whether he wins or loses. You will instil in him the understanding that love is not conditional on success, and he will internalise the idea that he is loveable and good regardless of what he can or can't do. The focus is on effort.

It's much easier to do well when you know your self-worth, and when your perceived worth to others doesn't rely on you being the number one footy pick or getting the top mark. If you think your credibility and value as a person depends on external markers such as these, a simple maths test to assess progress becomes much more high-stakes. You will feel that your value as a person is being put on the line every time you have to perform in some objective way.

For Prince Boofhead, each of his talents and exploits tend to be a source of self-esteem for his proud parents. Often, due to his parents' exhilaration about their son's considerable talents, their attention is drawn away from developing his internal, emotional competencies. This lack of attention to and cultivation of his internal world results in a boy with a desire to be the best but with limited ability to manage the shortfall between what he believes he can achieve (and is regularly told he can achieve) and what he *actually* achieves.

Prince Boofhead may even feel a sense of punishment (or shame) when he doesn't live up to expectations – this can wreak havoc on his self-esteem and send him into a downward spiral. He hasn't had the opportunity to learn that his parents will love him (and indeed that he is loveable) whether he 'wins' or 'loses'.

If your son seems deeply disappointed about the outcome of an activity, such as school grades or a sporting loss, make an effort to find something positive to comment on or have a discussion about what wasn't so good about the situation. He may have been feeling particularly anxious or unwell – and you acknowledging this will help.

Chapter 6

Maintain family rituals and traditions

A sense of belonging is a powerful human need. From an evolutionary point of view, being part of a group ensured our safety and survival, so this is why alienation is experienced as such a deep psychological threat. Indeed, people who feel that they are outsiders in their family, peer group or community are at greater risk of developing mental illness and engaging in antisocial behaviour than those with strong bonds.

While adolescents demand freedom and fight to attain it, they still need to feel that their family will be there if life gets overwhelming. And the stronger a family unit, the more confident a teenager will be that someone 'has their back'.

For Prince Boofhead, family disunity is often an important contributing factor to his feeling vulnerable. While his parents may be 'together' in the sense that they share an address, the reality is that they may spend very little time together due to extensive work or social commitments, or may have a very dysfunctional relationship.

They may also be separated or divorced, and possibly remarried to new partners.

So what builds strong families? The answer is shared positive experiences, plenty of communication and lots of family rituals and traditions.

A family tradition is pretty much anything a family does together proactively, as long as it's supported by some fanfare that lifts it above the monotonous routine of day-to-day life. It can be something as simple as watching home movies on birthdays. Or it can be repeated words or actions, special clothes or certain foods, TV shows or music. For example, it's not a tradition if you occasionally sit on the balcony and blow bubbles with your kids. But if you do it every Friday and then have Tim Tams and milk and call it your 'TGIF party', that's a family ritual. Other common rituals include the traditional Sunday roast, the Friday night feast for Shabbat in Jewish families, or attending a football match every Saturday afternoon. It doesn't matter what it is, as long as it makes the participants feel happy and more connected with their family.

Rituals can act as a countervailing force or psychological talisman against angry feelings of disconnection and disaffiliation. Cultural traditions can also provide children with a source of identity. In my family, for example, eating Sachertorte (chocolate and apricot cake) and Weihnachtsbäckerei (Austrian Christmas cookies) on Christmas Eve reminds me of my Austrian heritage.

RITUALS CHANGE AS CHILDREN GROW

In childhood, bedtime rituals were an important way to

help children feel safe and secure, and to help them wind down at the end of the day. In the preschool and early primary school years, all children benefit greatly from a nightly routine of bathing, brushing teeth, choosing a book and snuggling into bed while Mum or Dad reads the story to them. It helps them change gears from the hustle and bustle of family life to the stillness and solitude required for a good night's sleep.

Families use different types of rituals to celebrate key developmental transitions, such as starting primary or secondary school. For example, when each child in the family starts secondary school, they may be allowed to stay up later on Friday nights and join in the adults' film and popcorn night.

Equally, celebrating birthdays, anniversaries and holidays are important for many families. Going to a church, synagogue or mosque together at important times of the year can provide the psychological 'superglue' of the family; something consistent, stable and secure in a confusing world. These traditions and rituals help all members of the family make life cycle transitions and come together in times of crisis.

IT'S NEVER TOO LATE TO CREATE A FAMILY RITUAL

It is difficult to introduce new traditions in adolescence. Prince Boofhead wants to be with his friends, and thus he may well develop a crippling allergy to newly introduced family rituals or submit reluctantly to being involved.

But don't let this stop you. Teenagers may complain

and make a fuss about these rituals – but they'll usually be the first to complain and make a fuss if they are cancelled or don't occur. Family rituals and routines counteract the instability that is often evident in the teenage years during developmental transitions. Research shows that family rituals are associated with engaging in fewer risk behaviours, better social connection and better self-esteem in adolescence, and more secure attachment relationships in adulthood, as well as less depressive symptoms.

Below are some ideas for introducing rituals into a family with teenagers:

- Make the rituals align with the tasks that your teenager will need to do as an independent adult. For example, he can plan the evening meal for Saturdays and shop for groceries.
- Think about what already happens in the family and what may need just a little tweaking to turn it into a ritual. For example, the family may be able to take holidays at the same time of year at a place that is significant for them.
- Give presents that are reflective of the past year at birthdays or other important anniversaries, such as framing your son's signed grand final footy jumper.
- Have a pizza and movie night every Friday (does anyone *ever* grow out of this?).

Chapter 7
Set boundaries

You've probably seen them – young boys running wild through cafes and waiting rooms while their parents deflect their gaze to their phones and order another triple-shot skinny soy caramel macchiato. You've almost definitely heard them – little boys demanding, 'I want a ...' [insert battery-operated toy] or telling a parent who attempts to discipline them to 'Shut up!' You may even have stumbled across them – older boys smoking, drinking or shouting abuse in public.

Boys in particular seem to be biologically wired to seek out and push against boundaries. In fact, evolutionary biologists suggest that risk-taking males who display a tendency to break the rules are more desirable to females.

Adolescents will insist that they have the right to make their own decisions and that they are capable of judging when situations are dangerous, yet as we have seen, the part of the brain responsible for these executive functions is not developed until the mid twenties (and for some boys, it can be the late twenties). Boundaries are crucial for all adolescents because they help keep young people safe while their brains catch up with their bodies, and they provide the blueprint for developing their own internal standards of behaviour.

Yet when it comes to setting boundaries, many parents have lost the map *and* the compass. There seems to be a nationwide reluctance to use moral language. Whether this is because parents are fearful of their sons, are uncomfortable with discipline or perhaps just lack confidence, in many circumstances it appears that these boys have taken control of the household. Some parents only enforce limits when they or their sons are in danger. A key message in this book is that if parents don't develop the intestinal fortitude to set, maintain and consistently enforce clear limits, their sons will unrelentingly push until they meet resistance, usually in the form of outside agencies such as the school, the police or the judiciary system.

But setting limits doesn't mean becoming an authoritarian dictator meting out punishments left, right and centre; rather, it means having a developmental perspective and being consistent, firm, kind and fair.

BE A UNITED FRONT

The first step is to sit down with your partner (or with whomever you share parenting duties) and discuss the values you feel are important, particularly those relating to safety and respect. Then you need to agree on family rules that best reflect those values. For example, physical, verbal and emotional violence of any kind will not be tolerated.

You absolutely *must* have this conversation with your

co-parent first – even if you've been married for twenty years. There's no point opening a family rules discussion with your teenagers, only to find yourself arguing with your partner about curfews, alcohol consumption and video games. This sends a clear message that you are not on the same page, and any teen worth their salt will quickly take advantage of disunity.

The next step is to meet as a family to discuss the values of safety and respect, and to ask your tweens or teenagers to suggest rules that uphold these values. For example, 'We want to be safe' may lead them to suggest rules such as, 'Always tell a parent where we are going' or 'Never get in a car with a driver who has been drinking'. At this point, parents can guide the discussion to introduce the rules they have already discussed.

This kind of conversation works best before your son is in Year 7, but it can also work if he's older (it's just easier when they are younger). The key is for both you and your partner to be solidly, unwaveringly on the same page. Children are supremely gifted at playing parents against each other to find an escape clause – the old 'divide and conquer' strategy. If they have been successfully doing this all their lives, they won't suddenly stop in adolescence. If you and your partner make a weak team, do whatever it takes to marshal your forces. Get marriage counselling or go to dinner once a week to strengthen your connection. Disunity is toxic to effective parenting.

At 16, Dominic was an expert at manipulating his parents to get what he wanted. His father, George, had a very laid-back approach to discipline (a reaction against his own authoritarian father), while his mother, Rita, did her best to set some boundaries, but was undermined at every turn.

Dominic learned very quickly that if he wanted to do something risky (such as stay out all night at a party where kids were drinking and using drugs) all he had to do was wait until George was busy or preoccupied. He would then ask him at the last minute for permission to go, saying he was staying overnight 'at a mate's house' and off he went. Rita would hear from her husband that Dominic was staying with his friends and, although she knew that more information would have been appropriate, she lacked the courage to confront her husband or her son.

SET NON-NEGOTIABLE RULES

As we saw in Part 1, the key developmental goals in the adolescent years include breaking childhood bonds with parents, forming an identity and seeking independence. These are vital in answering the fundamental questions of the teenage years: Am I normal? Who am I? Where am I going? All this occurs against a backdrop of challenges: navigating the online world (including social media), attending parties where drugs and alcohol are available, and getting lifts with young and inexperienced drivers. A vital role for parents in this period is to set limits and boundaries that help teenagers develop in a safe and secure environment.

There are a million issues that parents of newly minted teenage boys may be confronted with. Maintaining your sanity means choosing which are the most important to you. While it is impossible to set strict rules about everything, you should have clearly articulated expectations about the issues that are the most crucial, namely those that are related to safety and respect towards both him and others. These are your parenting 'non-negotiables'.

Safety

These are rules relating to any behaviour that puts their health and wellbeing or that of others at risk. For example:

- A seatbelt must always be worn when riding in a car.
- A helmet must be worn when riding bikes and scooters.
- Violent, disrespectful and aggressive behaviour will not be tolerated.
- Bedtimes must be adhered to.
- No technology within 30 minutes of bedtime.
- There are time limits for online gaming or social networking.
- Alcohol or drug use is not acceptable.

Respect

These are rules relating to behaviour that disrespects them or others. For example:

- No name calling, teasing or bullying (online or offline).
- No posting of damaging material online.

- No destroying of property.
- No swearing.
- No physical abuse of others.

Given Prince's particular temperament, personality and level of emotional immaturity, I suggest that you err on the side of caution. Anything that relates to his safety has to be carefully discussed, and have rules set and consequences made crystal clear (if not chiselled on stone tablets). Then it is up to parents (both of them!) to do the monitoring, supervision and consistent enforcement.

> Our 14-year-old son knows that he always has to tell
> us where is he going and who he's going with, and that
> he must come home by an agreed time. Until recently,
> he was very good about following these rules. But then
> last weekend he not only got home an hour later than
> he said he would, but he also lied about where he'd
> been. I only found out because the mother of one of
> his friends saw the boys together and thought I should
> be informed. We haven't confronted him about his
> lying yet. How should we handle this?

It sounds as if you have neglected to agree on the consequences. It's a common mistake parents make – often because they are so psychologically frazzled after discussing the rules. Because your son is not sure what will happen if he doesn't follow the rules, he will try to get away with whatever he can. This is completely normal. Sit down with your son and be honest with him about the fact that you've found out what he did. Don't make a big deal about the lying. Instead, go over the rules again, this time agreeing on the consequences and enforcing them.

DON'T BRIBE YOUR CHILDREN

It may seem a reasonable way to 'encourage' children to do homework, eat vegetables and do chores around the house (especially when you consider the corporal punishment of days gone by), but rewarding children with money or material possessions has unwittingly created an army of mini materialists. And research indicates that using material possessions to express love and support leads to a societal acceptance that self-worth and the giving and receiving of love are tied to the accumulation of goods (hello hoarders). For example, 'If you don't buy me a new bike it means you don't really love me.'

When children follow the rules to get an external reward, it means they aren't internalising a code of behaviour – they're not following a rule because it adds to the greater good (e.g. helping a family, workplace or society protect its members), but because they want a reward. In the same way, children who follow the rules to avoid punishment are also denied an opportunity to develop a moral compass.

DISCUSS NEGOTIABLE RULES

After you have agreed on the non-negotiable rules and consequences, it's time to discuss the negotiable rules. These really depend on your personal and family values, which in turn may be influenced by particular cultural, religious or other beliefs. Negotiable rules may also need to be revised as a child matures and develops. And remember that one size does not fit all. All kids are different, so a rule that was appropriate for your 16-year-old boy may not be appropriate for your 16-year-old girl.

Some examples of negotiable rules may relate to:
- what your teenager elects to wear
- how he styles and colours his hair
- what movies and shows he watches
- how many streamed TV shows he watches per day
- what computer games he plays
- what music he listens to.

The goal in setting boundaries for negotiable matters is to help your teenager to make wise decisions on their own. So when you are discussing a particular rule, the smart move is to:
- initially reserve your parental opinion
- listen to what they want and give them time to say what they want and why
- in a very low key, matter-of-fact way review the pros and cons of their proposal and what the consequences might be if they mishandle the freedom that they're asking for.

My son is 15, and all of his friends are allowed to jump off the cliffs at the beach but we're not comfortable with that. We know that if we say no, he is just going to go and do it anyway and lie to us. What should we do?

It's interesting that you don't trust your son to tell you the truth. He may well sense that. Do some research and find out if this activity is as dangerous as you think. Then, try having a frank discussion with him about your concerns. Ask him why it is so important for him to do it. And genuinely listen. Tell him that you love him and that you are worried he may get really hurt. Ask him if he can think of a compromise that suits you both.

AGREE ON THE CONSEQUENCES

Parents will have the most success in setting limits if they allow their teenagers to have some say in the rules and what the consequences will be if these rules are broken. Conflict develops when authoritarian-style parents try to impose regulations without consulting their children. So at the same meeting that you discuss the non-negotiable rules, you also need to ask for your offspring's input on appropriate consequences for breaking them.

Sometimes parents worry that teenagers will come up with ridiculous consequences, but my experience is that most teenagers are very responsible when given the chance to take charge of aspects of their own lives.

My 14-year-old son is completely lazy. He never puts his washing in the laundry hamper, and he leaves food in his room and wet towels on the bedroom floor every single day. How can I encourage him to be more considerate of others and more responsible around the house?

No food in bedrooms should be a non-negotiable rule. Tell him it will encourage mice, rats and cockroaches (or any other vermin that give him the creeps). As for dirty washing, give your son his own laundry hamper and teach him to use the washing machine. This option comes with in-built consequences – if he doesn't do his own washing, he won't have clean clothes. As for the wet towels, if you leave them right where he drops them (instead of picking them up for him), he'll soon learn that it's best to take them back to the bathroom (especially if you hide all the other ones for a few days).

TIPS FOR TALKING TO BOYS

There is both art and science involved in successful communication with boys. Here are seven tried and true ways to improve your communication.

1. Give him prior notice of the conversation

If something has happened that you need to talk to him about, rather than just leaping in, warn him ahead of time that you would like to talk to him and give him a rough idea of what you want to talk about. For example, 'After dinner this evening, I'd like to talk about what happened with your sister last night.' It will give your son a heads-up, so he can gather his thoughts and come to the table prepared.

2. Run a check on your emotions

A few minutes prior to the discussion, check your mood – are you likely to become frustrated, tearful or angry? If so, you have two options. The first is to acknowledge your emotions. 'Hey I'm feeling a bit stressed out right now. Can we talk after dinner when I've calmed down?' This shows your son that feelings are normal and that your needs are important, too. This is particularly relevant for Prince Boofheads – he doesn't always come first, and now he knows it.

The alternative, if you don't feel up to the above, is to make an excuse and reschedule. 'Hey, I need to pick up something from the chemist – can we have that talk after dinner?'

If the conversation degrades into screaming or name-calling, there's no chance of getting the results you want. A perceived attack will only invoke a fight or flight response on the part of your teenager.

3. Make sure he's rested and fed

Make sure he's had enough sleep and has eaten before you start talking – after breakfast on the weekend might be a good time. You're less likely to receive irritated and grouchy responses to your questions. Also, make sure he is not affected by drugs or alcohol (or hungover). Talking to an inebriated teen is like swimming in treacle.

4. Move while you talk

Boys think best when they are active and mobile, so it might be best to ditch the intense conversation across the table and take him to the park to kick a ball or go for a bike ride around the neighbourhood. The outside environment is likely to keep him alert and engaged, and it also takes the conversation away from routine life. Most teenage boys will also be much more comfortable with the limited direct eye contact involved in such situations.

5. Refrain from a lecture

A long-winded monologue outlining all of his faults and what he did wrong is not going to work. Make a short list of the points you wish to get across, in order of importance. Give him a chance to respond to each point before moving on, even if it is simply a grunt of acknowledgement – at least this shows that he is listening.

6. Give him concrete examples

Making a vague reference to the state of his bedroom or his attitude or lack of respect isn't going to mean much to your son. Use physical or concrete requests or examples:

- 'Please bring uneaten food out of your bedroom and place it in the bin.'
- 'When you don't thank me for driving you and your friends to and from soccer training every week, it makes me feel resentful and I don't really want to do it any more.'

And remember the golden rule – choose your battles. Save your energy for the big stuff.

7. Follow up the conversation

It may seem as though the conversation was pointless – after all, he didn't really say much or just seemed to say what you wanted to hear. But don't despair – it may take him a little while to process the conversation. Look out for examples where he may have changed the way he did something based on your discussion, and subtly but positively reinforce his efforts.

SUPERVISE AND MONITOR

It's not enough to simply set limits and boundaries. As we've seen, teenagers are yet to develop the cognitive ability to reliably and consistently assess a situation and make good decisions. You need to continue to play a navigation role in their lives, and this is where supervision and monitoring is critical. As Joanne Fedler explains in *Love in the Time of Contempt: Consolations for Parents of Teenagers*, parents need to be interested but not excessively curious about their teenagers' lives; to have their backs without hovering.

The inverse relationship between supervision and risky behaviour in the teenage years is nicely illustrated by a US study by Kenneth H. Beck and his colleagues. To examine the relationship between parental monitoring and adolescent alcohol use, they asked teenagers to complete a survey at baseline and 12 months later. They found that highly monitored teenagers were less likely to report drinking alcohol 12 months later. A more recent study by researchers at the National Drug and Alcohol Research Centre at the University of New South Wales backs up this finding. They examined drinking behaviour in nearly 2000 teenagers and their parents over four years, starting in Year 7. The study indicated that parental monitoring was one of several factors that were instrumental in preventing early drinking. Other factors included positive family relationships, a religious background and alcohol-specific rules.

This is largely common sense. If you are a teenager whose parents routinely know where you are, who you are with and what you are doing, then on the balance of probabilities there will be less opportunity to participate in risky behaviour. Conversely, the study also found that parental supply of alcohol doubled the likelihood that the teenager would be drinking full serves of alcohol a year later, and made it *fifteen times* more likely that they would drink alcohol acquired from other sources. So if you think that providing alcohol in a controlled environment will stop your son from drinking elsewhere – think again.

> Karin knew something wasn't quite right when her 16-year-old son, James, quit his guitar lessons and gave up playing in the school band. She put it down to him 'being a teenager' and that he was probably struggling a bit because he had only just hit puberty. She also thought his moodiness, extreme need for privacy and unwillingness to communicate were also just normal adolescent behaviour, so she tried not to take his rudeness personally. Her relationship with him up until this point had been very open and they had regularly talked about many things. She held on to this connection and trusted him to make good decisions, rarely interrogating his plans. Her partner, Stephen, was a passive and uninvolved parent who worked long hours and spent very little time with his son.

James barely needed to raise a sweat in formulating a story that his mother would believe (his father never asked), while he confidently went about conducting his social life as he pleased.

If Karin ever called or texted James to find out where he was, he never answered or replied. And when he returned the next morning, he would claim his 'phone had run out of charge', or he 'had no credit'. Everything changed when Stephen received a call from the police station, saying James had been caught with some boys who were tagging (the form of graffiti where boys spray their gang or individual 'tags' on public property). Both parents were deeply shocked by James's behaviour and realised they needed to work together to help him make better choices.

As much as Prince Boofhead despises being controlled and monitored, his parents simply cannot afford to forgo supervision, particularly with his personality and drama-seeking temperament. No amount of carping and whingeing on his part can change the fact that his prefrontal cortex requires adequate time to fully develop and, until then, decision-making, impulse control, risk assessment and good judgement are all traits that are still under construction. Prince Boofhead *needs* his parents to take control – whether he likes it or not.

In an iteration of the words of psychologist Sean Grover, children are not born leaders – they learn how to lead themselves by being guided by engaged parents who see them as independent beings, not the other way around.

Chapter 8
Learn to say 'no'

'No.' Such a tiny word, yet so powerful when used effectively and appropriately. For example:

- 'Can I have those ($300) jeans?' *No.*
- 'Can I go to my friend's 16th birthday party (where the parents are providing a keg)?' *No.*
- 'Can I eat in my bedroom?' *No.*
- 'Can I watch the movie (that's rated MA and I'm nine years old)?' *No.*
- 'Can I stay at my mate's house (whose parents are not home)?' *No.*

When your son is asking to break a non-negotiable rule (see page 59), a firm and respectful 'no' affirms your authority. There is no need for an apology or for long-winded explanations. He knows the rules. A simple 'no', delivered in an even tone tells him that you are confident in your decision to limit his behaviour, but that you still respect him.

For negotiable rules, make sure both you and your

partner (where applicable) are there to discuss your child's request, and keep the explanation for your answer as short and simple as possible. The longer he keeps you talking, the greater his chances of finding a flaw in your argument and wearing you down.

And if he keeps hammering you with different reasons why he should be able to get what he wants, simply repeat your answer – aka the famous broken record technique. However, if he is getting upset, it is important to acknowledge his feelings using 'and' instead of 'but'. For example:

- 'I can see that you are upset about this, and the answer is still no.'
- 'I understand how hard it is to miss out on something you really want, and the answer is no.'
- 'I can hear how disappointed you are, and the answer is still no.'

Each time we say 'no', we are giving our children the opportunity to develop emotional intelligence – the ability to handle their feelings of disappointment, anger and frustration when things don't go their way. Being able to get over their disappointment allows them to think of more creative solutions to problems – which encourages resilience.

Moreover, by modelling how to say 'no', we show our children how to do this too, which is crucial for their moral development. It means they can say, 'No, I don't want to' when someone is asking them to do something they feel is wrong. We all want to raise responsible, considerate, cooperative children who do the right thing, but that doesn't imply blind obedience. Morality is doing what's right, no matter what you're told; obedience is doing what you're told, no matter what's right.

As a parent, your goal is to do yourself out of a job – to raise a human being who respects himself and others, and who is capable of taking care of himself. Your goal is not to be your child's best friend or to be popular. Sometimes this means saying no and riding out the response. And while it'll be a hell of a lot harder to say no to Prince Boofhead now he is a young adult, there will be times when it will still be appropriate. You may just have to weather a Category 5 cyclone rather than a storm.

Here is a seven-step plan for parent–teenager negotiation:

1. The parent or teenager makes a request or suggestion.
2. The other person shares their reaction, without saying yes or no to the request or suggestion.
3. Each person then outlines specific issues/problems with the request or suggestion.
4. Both parties brainstorm solutions to the problems raised.
5. If there is agreement, the negotiation is over.
6. If there is no agreement, both parties try to find a compromise.
7. If no compromise is apparent, then state differing positions as objectively and respectfully as possible and decide on a time to try again.

DON'T CAVE IN

Once you have said 'no', it is crucial that you stick to your guns. Children become adept at pestering, pleading and whining from an early age, but will only continue this behaviour if parents have occasionally relented. Dr David Walsh, author of *No: Why Kids – of All Ages – Need to Hear It and Ways Parents Can Say It* refers to it as a 'well rehearsed routine' where the child makes a scene and the parent quickly caves in after a brief attempt to hold their ground.

'Kia kaha' is a Maori phrase that means *stay strong*. This is easier said than done, especially when you are confronted by a nonstop querulous, tired, hormonal, cantankerous, grouchy son or when your in-laws are looking all 'judgey' when said son is doing a commendable imitation of the eruption of Mount Vesuvius. But we teach people how to treat us. If you relent, just as the sun will rise tomorrow morning, nothing is more certain than that you will be setting yourself up for a shitstorm of more obnoxious and demanding behaviour later on. If you're unswervingly solid, sturdy and robust in parenting a Prince Boofhead, especially in early adolescence, it will eventually dawn on them that such behaviour is ultimately pointless in helping them get what they want at home or out of life.

Next time your son erupts, try 'faking it til you make it' – pretending to be self-assured in who you are and what you want to accomplish as a parent, even if you don't feel it. (See chapter 9 for more on emotional intelligence.)

Jessie's tantrums became family folklore. If he didn't
get his way, everyone within a hundred kilometres
would hear about it. As many parents will sympathise,
when your child is throwing a toxic tantrum in public,
you may feel an urge to do whatever it takes to help
them calm down. In Jessie's case, his parents, particularly his mother, found it so difficult to manage his
behaviour that she soon felt scared to ever say no.
In fact, his mother and father deftly anticipated or
shielded their son from any threats of disappointment.

If this pattern of behaviour continues, Jessie's parents
will be setting up a difficult time in his adolescence and
beyond. Since Jessie has rarely had to face any disappointments or negative events, he'll struggle to deal with
these things when they inevitably occur in everyday life
outside the home.

WHAT IF YOU CAN'T SAY NO?

Given it is so important for children to be told no, why
do so many parents struggle to say it? The short answer
is fear – fear of their child's rage, disappointment and
hatred. 'I hate you!' 'You are so unfair!' 'Everyone else gets
to do what they want!' In other words, we cannot cope
when they express strong negative feelings towards us.
Some parents also tell me that they don't want to say no
because they fear that their child will miss out and that
this will create deep psychological scars. In fact, as we've
already seen, the opposite is true – it is the experience of
repeatedly *not* missing out that creates the psychological

scars. So what is going on here? If we dig a little deeper, we find a harsh truth – if parents themselves are not very resilient, they will be pushing the proverbial shit uphill when it comes to saying no to their children.

Resilience is not about being brave or strong, it is about being able to get back on the horse. It's about being willing to put yourself in the position of a student – to be open to trying something new and to ask for help if you need it. At its core, it is feeling okay about yourself, and knowing that you will get through whatever happens in your life.

In my experience, parents who do not feel happy in their primary relationship, are unfulfilled at work or have unresolved issues from their own childhoods will often find it harder to disappoint their children. These parents mean well, but their own need for love and approval is so overpowering that they will put their need for their son to like them before their son's need to learn to like himself.

All parents need to know what they bring to their parenting experience. We all have a 'family of origin', whether biological, adoptive or some other collection of significant others who fed, clothed and sheltered us and taught us about relationships, emotions and life. What many people fail to recognise is that these early experiences have a major influence on how we see ourselves and others, how we cope with daily life and how we parent.

Kathy always found it difficult to soothe her son Ben. Looking back now, she thinks it may have had something to do with how quickly she went back to work after he was born. She loved him, but she also loved her job, and her mixture of guilt and fear meant she could not bear to hear him cry. As he grew, she found herself caving in to his every demand. Ben became emotionally dependent on his father, Yuri, who became more of a friend than a parent. This produced a developmental problem for Ben: a lack of genuine confidence to emancipate from either parent.

In Year 10, Ben enrolled in a Year 11 subject and appeared grandiose and overconfident about his abilities. But when it came to the exam for this subject, he became extremely stressed. Instead of being able to acknowledge his discomfort with the challenge, he became angry and took out his rage on those around him, including his mother and father. He would fly into a rage if asked to do something he didn't like, and was rude and oppositional to his parents and dismissive of their offers to help. On occasions he would punch holes in walls and throw objects around his room. Kathy was terrified of these outbursts and would depend on Yuri to step in and calm Ben down.

It's not unusual for a father or mother to provide reassurance for teens who are facing a challenge, but for Prince Boofheads like Ben, the frequent meltdowns (and consequent crisis management) are always out of proportion to the impending event. By never letting him experience disappointment at a young age, Kathy and Yuri had unwittingly prevented their son from learning how to manage his fear of failure.

Chapter 9
Encourage emotional intelligence

Emotional intelligence is the ability to recognise and express our emotions without damaging our connections with others. And like all key socio-emotional skills, our children learn to do this by watching us. In other words, 'monkey see, monkey do'. If, every time something doesn't go right in your life, you tend to overreact and throw a temper tantrum, then the odds are a) that your son has watched you from a young age and b) that he will respond to frustration in the same way. Boys tend to regulate their emotions in exactly the same way as their parents regulate theirs.

MANAGE YOUR OWN ANGER

It's natural to feel angry at our children, even furious. But we are the adults – our job is to control the expression of our anger and therefore minimise its negative impact. This isn't always easy, especially when we're flooded with fight or flight hormones and our muscles are tense, our pulse is racing, our breath quickens and we're ready to either clobber someone or run a marathon. No matter how hard it is to stay calm at these moments, we know that the last thing we want to do is hurt our kids. We need to walk away, take time out or remove ourselves from the situation so that we don't hit, swear, use name-calling or sarcasm or scream at our kids. When your kids watch you deal constructively with your anger, they'll learn how to handle their own. You'll become a role model for your child, showing them that anger is part of being human, and that learning to manage anger responsibly is part of becoming mature.

The next time someone cuts you off in traffic, there's no gas in the barbecue or someone knocks over the garbage bin you placed lovingly on the kerb, stay calm by taking a few deep breaths or going for a walk.

However, if the people you love say that outbursts of rage are a repeated pattern of behaviour for you, it's important to seek some coping strategies from a mental health professional or check out the tips at: www.psychology.org.au/publications/tip_sheets/anger.

APOLOGISE IF YOU LOSE YOUR TEMPER

One of the greatest gifts you can give your son is to admit you've stuffed up, and to apologise. Some parents (particularly dads) have trouble with this. They rationalise that if they say sorry, they are giving up power or displaying weakness.

The key is to ask yourself what it is you want to teach your son about adult relationships. Surely we want our boys to know when they've screwed up and teach them the importance of a heartfelt apology. Modelling this type of humility shows our sons that we are all human and that there is no such thing as a perfect parent.

But an even better strategy is to defuse a tense situation before you lose your temper in the first place. This is another important skill your son needs to learn. So what are the most effective ways to defuse heated arguments before they cascade out of control? Here are three steps for defusing an argument:

1. Put your judgement temporarily on ice (easier said than done, especially if you feel that you are being ill-treated, abused or misrepresented). Do some deep breathing, which triggers the relaxation response – most of us physically tense up during arguments and tensing up is like pouring kerosene on the fires of your frustration. You can call a momentary time-out if you're feeling overwhelmed. 'I need to pee – be back in a sec . . .'
2. Once you have calmed down, inform your son that you really want to have a better understanding of his point of view. To really hear his perspective, you must park your ego and resist the temptation to jump in with an observation or comment. Again, this is about faking it until you make it; convince your son that you are genuine in your attempt to understand why he is so angry – is it fear, hurt or frustration or a combination of all three?
3. Look for a grain of truth in your son's view. There is usually some truth to some of his argument. Maybe

someone has been thoughtless, unkind or cruel in some way. Whatever the case, your son's viewpoint feels totally acceptable to him and trying to debate this will only increase the emotional temperature. So instead, put a sock in it, listen carefully and work towards empathy rather than launching a counter-offensive.

Most teenage boys will respond well to feeling understood, especially by the people they are closest to. Injecting statements that indicate to him that he has been heard and understood can dramatically reduce the intensity of the argument, paving the way to healthier and more effective communication.

LISTEN RESPECTFULLY

I've never met a boy who didn't want recognition that his thoughts and feelings mattered and were being taken seriously. As a parent, your job is to use your fully developed adult brain (with its wired-up 100 billion brain cells) to figure out what lies behind the words and actions of your offspring. This does not mean caving in to every outrageous demand, but calmly listening and then asserting the simple fact that no-one on the planet can behave any way they want, all of the time. As we saw in chapter 3, your average teenage boy pushes you away just when he needs you most – and high on the list of what he needs from you is the feeling of safety and security that comes from knowing you will enforce the discussed and agreed-upon rules. Calmly asserting our authority with our sons is one of the purest forms of love.

WHAT IF MY TEENAGE SON IS REALLY ANGRY?

When your son is upset and acting out, avoid the temptation to scream like a banshee. Instead, try taking a deep breath, listening without interrupting, and acknowledging how they feel. This way, they'll know you're listening and that you take their concerns seriously.

- DON'T try to reason with, problem-solve, negotiate or deliver a lecture on conflict resolution or anger management to your son when he is angry.
- DO give him space.
- DON'T attempt to physically restrain, hug, cuddle or in any other way invade his space while he remains angry.
- DO empathise, then walk away. Make a statement like, 'I can see you're upset – let's talk about this later' – then remove yourself from their immediate vicinity.
- DO follow up when things have calmed down, to discuss what happened, what went wrong and how it could be different next time.
- DO look after yourself. Being verbally abused by a teenage boy can be draining. Make sure you debrief with a partner or a friend. (See page 159 for what to do if the abuse becomes physical.)

ALLOW BOREDOM

In these days of overscheduling our children to attempt to give them the 'edge', we risk not allowing them to draw on their own resources to occupy themselves. Boredom is not a negative thing. Your child needs periods of time when they have no commitments.

Unstructured time can give your son the opportunity to seek out new experiences and pursue what sparks his interest. This might lead him to build something, learn a new skill by watching YouTube videos, write a story, organise friends to make a video, or simply study the ants marching into the kitchen.

Unstructured time can enhance all aspects of his development and help him develop a positive self-image. And when others are involved, he can learn new social skills. More importantly, the experience of deciding for himself how to use periods of unstructured time teaches him how to do it well. One of our biggest challenges as adults, and even as teenagers, is learning to manage our time well.

So if your child is younger and regularly complains about being bored, don't cave in to filling the gap. Resist the temptation to hand over the iPad. A parent's response to the words 'I'm bored' should be to repeat the unofficial slogan of the US Marine Corps in the face of any adversity: 'Improvise, adapt, overcome.' Regardless of who we are or what we do, our ability to put these three words into practice is the framework for success.

If you can't imagine yourself saying, 'Improvise, adapt, overcome,' then keep it simple: 'Well, that's a shame.'

Leave him in silence and watch as his mind becomes quiet and his internal self takes over. In the end, all we have is our imagination. If something cannot be made up in your mind first – be it a painting, book, relationship or cure for cancer – it can't exist. We are ultimately bound by what we can imagine.

You are not able to upload inventiveness, ingenuity or imagination into your son, but you can and should do everything in your power to provide him with an environment where his creativity is supported, not just another mess to clean up. It *is* possible for boredom to deliver a child his best self, the one that searches for exciting ideas and brilliance. If he sits still long enough, he may hear the bid behind boredom. So let him sit. With practice, he may develop the resourcefulness to rise up and respond.

Max and his parents seemed to be caught up in an endless cycle of fighting. Ever since he could remember, there had been a calendar on the fridge that outlined all of his commitments for the week – tennis, cricket, homework, guitar lessons and so on. The calendar was a sea of multi-coloured markers with no gaps. Max felt so stressed every time he looked at it. He just wanted some time to chill, play a video game and muck around once in a while. But instead, all he ever did was fight with his father about doing music practice or with his mother about why he could never find his tennis gear. Eventually, he admitted to his parents that he did not want to continue playing tennis. His parents were not happy (given the amount of money and time they had invested), but Max was desperate to try to find some unscheduled time to relax and do nothing.

MODEL EMPATHY

Empathy is the ability to recognise and appreciate another person's feelings and to see things from their point of view. It is something we learn through our relationships with our primary caregivers and enables us to build strong connections with the people in our lives. By the age of two, most toddlers begin to realise that they are separate individuals and will sometimes offer to help other children (or adults), though it is usually something that *they* find helpful. For example, they might (adorably) give someone who is upset a bottle or a blanket. It's not until the age of six or seven that they will understand what another person might find helpful, and it takes until adolescence for children to begin to empathise with wider societal issues such as discrimination.

However, children need help to develop empathy, and they get that by being around adults who are caring and compassionate. Every time you say thank you, apologise after you lose your temper, remember someone's birthday, or do some volunteering or donate to charity, your children are absorbing it all like little sponges. They are watching how you do it and, especially, noticing that it makes you feel good.

Positive psychology research indicates that caring about other people is fundamental to our happiness in both the short and long term. In fact, research has found that children whose parents engage in philanthropy (such as donating or raising money for charity or volunteering in the community) report increased levels of physical and psychological wellbeing in adulthood.

At 13, Antonio was remarkably selfish. He refused to use his pocket money to buy gifts for anyone, and never offered to share food or snacks with other children, even though his parents always gave him excessive amounts of food and extra lunch money every day. But he wasn't born like this. Like all children, he needed encouragement to develop his innate ability to empathise with others and to learn to care about what happened to them. At two, Antonio, like all toddlers, would engage in 'parallel play' – playing alongside others, but not with them. He was focused on himself and his toys and was not even able to think about what others wanted or felt. Things only went pear-shaped when he wanted a toy that another child had, or a playmate wanted his 'favourite' toy. Then all hell would break loose. Unfortunately, his mother was afraid of his tantrums, so she made sure there were so many toys in his toy box that sharing with other children seldom became an issue. This meant she did not have to use distraction, which would help him engage the thinking part of his brain ('Let's find a better toy') or to model empathy ('Thank you for sharing. Look how happy the other little boy is!').

As he grew older, Antonio did not see the value in sharing, and was always protected from having to experience jealousy, anger or frustration. The result was a classic Prince Boofhead, who had no respect for his parents, had a lack of gratitude and a strong sense of entitlement, and who behaved in a controlling manner, had a bad temper, was insensitive to family members and peers, absolutely refused to help around the house and was excessively angry when things didn't go his way.

PRACTISE GRATITUDE

In chapter 2, I talked about teaching children the difference between wants and needs, and how acts of kindness and philanthropy help us to be grateful for what we have. This simple, five-minute ritual can be completed as a family every day, perhaps after dinner. Simply share three things that you are grateful for or that went well during the day and why you feel good about them. Doing it together is great for younger children as it models positive thinking and emotional intelligence. It shows them how to focus on what went right rather than dwelling on what went wrong. Even on a really bad day, inevitably something good happens, however tiny (e.g. reading a few pages of a great book).

If you have older children, you can modify the activity by writing down what went well every day, and then having a look at your progress over several weeks. You can do the first one together as a family, and then leave everyone to do their own.

To make it work, the following four components are essential:

- Regularity – it must be done every night.
- Recording – it needs to be written down (so you can reflect on it later).
- Questioning – for each of the three things, think about why you feel good about it. This may feel a little weird at first, but keep trying.
- Reflect – after a week, look back on what you have written. Are there any themes?

You can encourage your teenage son to try this for a week at first and see what he thinks. Suggest that he keep going for another couple of weeks at least. It may end up being a bedtime habit, or he may find he doesn't need to do it every night.

That's it. We spend thousands of dollars on expensive electronics, homes, cars and holidays, hoping to feel happier. This is a free alternative, and it works.

In a study of the technique's effectiveness, Professor Martin Seligman, the acknowledged 'father' of the positive psychology movement, asked participants to follow these exact instructions for one week. The results showed that after one week the participants were 2 per cent happier. Participants continued using the technique, and follow-up tests showed that reported happiness levels increased to 5 per cent after one month and to 9 per cent after six months.

Chapter 10

My top tips for raising resilient, empathetic boys

Babies don't arrive in this world arrogant, lacking empathy or with a chronic sense of entitlement. In fact, we are all born with an innate tendency towards social bonding, kindness and concern for others. Knowing that the environment has a major impact on how our children develop into young adults – that we teach people how to treat us – we need to start modelling resilience and empathy and cultivating these qualities in our children. Here are my top tips for raising resilient, empathetic boys:

1. Show your son that you love him whether he wins or loses. Praise effort as well as achievement. Self-esteem is stronger and deeper when a child realises their self-worth doesn't hinge on perfection and, better still, that a slight mistake or failure doesn't render him useless. If he sees himself as loveable and good regardless of what he can or can't do, he will do the same in his own relationships.

2. Let your boys experience adversity. Let them learn that they *can* handle it and, in the process, develop

compassion for themselves and others.

3. Foster a relationship with a supportive, charismatic adult. It could be an uncle, a family friend, a coach, or a trusted teacher. All boys who do well have one of these relationships.

4. Let him take responsibility for his contribution to disappointing outcomes. Symptoms of not being able to take responsibility include the infuriating trait of changing the goalposts in a conversation, rather than acknowledging and taking responsibility for what has been said or done. Make sure you are not guilty of doing this either!

5. Be your own hero. Make sure there is enough going on in your own life that you are not living vicariously through your son's. For Prince Boofhead, each of his talents and exploits is also a source of self-esteem for his proud parents. Instead, he needs you to focus on his internal, emotional experiences. Be careful, though, if he is used to only receiving praise for his exploits. If this changes, he may perceive the shift as a punishment or evidence that he isn't good enough. Use your words wisely.

6. Never put up with intimidating or violent behaviour, even if it seems trivial or insignificant (see page 159). Communicate with him in a calm manner that is not belittling, patronising or condescending. Help him learn to solve problems without using aggression.

7. If violence, mental illness and substance abuse are interfering with normal adolescent development

and family safety, seek professional help from a psychologist, mental health professional or family support service. Family support and connections make a vital different to outcomes at this stage of development.

Part 3

Common issues

In Part 1 we looked at how a child's early experiences may contribute to the development of Prince Boofhead Syndrome. Part 2 examined the strategies parents can implement to help their sons develop greater emotional resilience. In this section, I will explore some of the key issues that may arise for Prince Boofheads and what you can do to minimise damage to their health and wellbeing.

Chapter 11
Sleep, eat, move, repeat

Since positive peer relationships are crucial to young people's wellbeing, one might think that all the texting, social media, video-game playing and imbibing that our boys are engaging in suggests they're doing okay. However, while most of our boys look healthy on the outside, there's now a truckload of evidence to suggest that the physical wellbeing of our young people is actually at an all-time low. Data suggests that, as a nation, Australia is dropping the ball when it comes to the fundamental building blocks of wellbeing – namely sleep, diet and exercise. As parents, we are often far more focused on issues such as smoking, drugs and sex than we are on fundamentals such as sleep, nutrition and exercise.

A GOOD NIGHT'S SLEEP

If you're an average person, around 36 per cent of your life will be spent asleep, which is the equivalent of 32 years in the life of a 90-year-old. It must be pretty important to take up that much time, yet sleep deprivation is reaching epidemic proportions in today's fast-paced society. In the 1950s, most adults reported around eight hours of sleep a night. Nowadays we're more likely to report around six hours or fewer.

For teenagers, it's often worse. These days, my teenage male clients don't seem to be getting enough sleep; in fact, if sleep deprivation were an Olympic sport, Australia would get a place on the insomnia podium. Teenage boys seem to be in the grip of a creeping epidemic of irritability, accident-proneness and chronic health conditions as modern lifestyles interfere with the primal wiring of their internal body clocks. While the research is clear that they need around nine hours of sleep for optimal brain performance, many of them are only getting around 5–6 hours on a school night. This is not enough to function well, let alone tackle the challenges of the final years of school.

The dilemma for teenagers, however, is this: when your teenage boy finds it hard to get out of bed in the morning and hard to fall asleep at night, he's not just being lazy or difficult. The release of melatonin, which is the hormonal messenger that announces the arrival of darkness (and hence bedtime) to our brains, is delayed from puberty onwards. To put it simply, because of the biology of human development, the sleep mechanism in adolescent boys does not allow the brain to naturally awaken before about 8 a.m. At the other end of the day, they often don't feel tired until late in the evening (after 11 p.m.). So unless their school is a 5-minute walk from home, getting up in the morning on a weekday is always going to be a problem.

As many as 80 per cent of teenagers report being sleepy when they wake up, which impacts their ability to function well at school. Many teenagers end up chronically sleep deprived as a result, with all the accompanying outcomes of this, including irritability and poor concentration.

Sleep has two crucial functions:

- *Cellular growth and repair.* Sleep allows the body to repair and grow muscles and tissues, and rejuvenate itself. The restoration theory has gained support from empirical evidence collected in human and animal studies. The most striking of these comes from the work of Carol Everson who, in 1989, discovered that rats deprived of sleep lose all immune function and die within 2–3 weeks.

- *Brain processing and memory consolidation.* In the case of the latter, it's not just about creating memories and being able to recall them when needed. Sleep is so powerful that our ability to solve complex problems is greatly enhanced by a good night's sleep. The most important neural connections are linked and strengthened by sleep, while others that are needed less fade away. Research also shows that creativity is enhanced when we first emerge from sleep – that is, first thing in the morning.

If your son has been studying hard but deprives himself of sleep in the process, the ability to retain what he has learned is significantly diminished. Instead, 'sleeping on it' allows the brain to consolidate and clarify what he has learned. The brain in sleep is less constrained by the conscious focus on particular things during the day, and is free to 'wander' and find new and useful connections that link together to propose novel solutions.

The main message here is to take sleep seriously. We used to intuitively understand the importance of sleep, but now it's a badge of honour to resist it. The sleep message is not some sort of crystal-waving mantra; it's a pragmatic response for good health. Good sleep habits are associated with increased concentration, better attention, good decision-making, creativity and sociability. It reduces mood changes, stress, anger levels, impulsivity and alcohol and drug use. More recent research is exploring how sleep is associated with mental illness and is providing new ways of treating these often debilitating conditions.

TIPS FOR IMPROVING SLEEP

Here are a number of suggestions for helping your son improve his sleep.

Encourage him to go to bed and wake up at the same time each day

Having a regular bedtime and wake time helps to set the body clock. As well as a morning alarm, it may be useful to set an alarm to alert him when it is bedtime.

Make his bedroom a haven for sleep

Bedrooms need to be as dark as possible at night, and slightly cool. Make sure any digital clock faces are pointed away from the bed. Use the bed only for sleeping – not lying in bed to watch TV. If he is feeling anxious or worried, get him to put a pad and pen beside his bed and scribble down any anxious thoughts before falling asleep.

Reduce light exposure at least half an hour before bed

Melatonin is triggered by darkness, so light inhibits its production. Yet one of the last things we do before we go to bed is stand in our brightly lit bathrooms and brush our teeth, just after shutting down the computer. Think about what can be changed to ensure light exposure is as low as possible.

Ban technology from the bedroom

Turn off mobile phones, iPads and laptops and anything else that is going to excite the brain at least an hour before bedtime. Read a book instead. A 2014 study by Brigham and Women's Hospital in Boston showed that night-time iPad readers took longer to fall asleep and felt less sleepy at night compared with people who were assigned print books. Enforce a 'no technology in the bedroom' rule – devices should be switched off and left to charge in a public place. That means everybody's devices – be a good role model.

Wind down

Create an evening ritual for the family where everyone is expected to wind down for at least a few minutes before bed. Play some quiet, relaxing music, turn off lights and wind down conversation. Learn relaxation and deep breathing techniques. Do whatever will help ease you into the 'honey-heavy dew of slumber'. Exercise is a good sleep inducer – but only if it is done at least two hours before bedtime.

If he can't sleep, get him to do something else

If sleep is evasive, tell him to get out of bed and go and do something in another room, such as reading or playing a game of Solitaire (with real playing cards, not a computer!). Then he can return to bed when he is feeling drowsy.

Limit caffeine, alcohol and nicotine intake

Although caffeine tends to affect people in different ways, ideally it's best to avoid drinking any caffeinated drinks, including energy drinks, after lunch. Researchers in Israel have found that drinking coffee halves the body's levels of melatonin (the sleep hormone), and that study participants slept less well after quaffing a cup of coffee than after drinking the same amount of decaf. On average, subjects slept five-and-a-half hours per night after drinking caffeinated coffee, compared with seven hours after decaf.

Nicotine, like caffeine, is also a stimulant, so it interferes with sleep quality. Although alcohol helps us fall asleep, it's usually poor quality sleep (less REM) and we're also more likely to wake up in the middle of the night or too early the next morning. This is due to the fluctuation in adenosine (a sleep-inducing chemical in the brain), which increases rapidly after we drink, but then subsides again.

Seek out morning light

Light exposure in the morning shuts down the production of melatonin and sets the biological clock to the light–dark cycle.

Use technology to improve sleep

There are different types of technology available that may help your son improve his sleep, including wearable technology and smartphone apps. The interaction with technology may pique his interest and encourage him to sleep more. For example, the Jawbone UP3 is a slim wristband that monitors activity and sleep. It tracks deep sleep, light sleep and REM sleep, and provides tips to help get a better night's rest, one night at a time.

Other biometric devices include the Fitbit Flex2, which automatically tracks how long and how well the wearer sleeps, sets a sleep goal and bedtime reminder to form good habits, and will wake the wearer peacefully with a silent alarm. It can also wirelessly sync the data to a computer and smartphone.

Recharge is a personalised six-week program accessed via a smartphone app that can help your teenager improve his general health and wellbeing by focusing on four key areas, including:

- helping him establish a regular wake and sleep time each day
- fun activities triggered by an alarm clock designed

to get him up and out of bed
- increasing his exposure to daylight early in the day, to help reset his body clock
- encouraging him to increase his physical activity, especially within two hours of waking up.

Your son will receive practical tips to improve his sleep–wake routine and wellbeing, daily reports to track his mood, energy, exercise and sleep, and graphs to help monitor his progress, which can be reviewed in each session.

NUTRITIOUS FOOD

The sheer volume of food that can be consumed by a teenage boy, especially after school, comes as a shock to most parents. Chances are that your teenage son has either eaten all his lunch by the end of recess or elected to play sport instead of eating at all. It may feel to you like a neverending cycle of shop, cook, eat and clean. And forget the childhood tricks of small, individualised portions of chips or muesli bars — adolescence calls for the heavy artillery.

Add a couple more teenagers to the house and the local supermarket will be buying you a specially made oversized trolley. It may start to look a little like the case study below.

Shona has two teenage boys: Jonathan, 15, and Stuart, 17. The boys have different tastes in food, which can be difficult to juggle, especially since she is accused of favouritism when she makes one or the other's favourite meals. Stuart is quite conscious of his diet and is constantly trawling websites to see what new advice is available. It's hard for Shona to keep up: one week she bought 5 litres of milk to keep pace with Stuart's demands, only to discover that he had found a website that said to avoid milk if you want to increase your muscle bulk. When she stopped buying it, he complained about there being no milk. Shona's kitchen is never tidy as both boys eat constantly, even though she tries to keep it to three meals a day. Last night Jonathan ate half a roast chicken, two bread rolls, a 1-kilogram tub of vanilla yoghurt and a punnet of strawberries an hour before dinner and then said he wasn't hungry when dinner was served. Shona dutifully refrigerated the leftovers, which Jonathan promptly claimed as his own, saying, 'It was my dinner.' All hell broke loose the next day when Jonathan wandered into the kitchen after a sleep-in to find that Stuart had eaten the leftovers.

Unfortunately, in this case, Shona has made a rod for her own back. Since Shona bears the weighty responsibility of doing all the shopping and cooking (without any help from her husband or sons), she gets to make the rules. And one of her rules should be no 'vacuuming' the fridge within two hours of a main meal, with the consequence that rule breakers get to pay for their own groceries and cook their own meals.

How to encourage healthy eating habits

- DON'T worry excessively about your son's diet. Overall, as long as teenage boys are healthy and active, there's no great need to police their food intake too strictly. If your son, however, is not very active, steer clear of foods high in refined flour and sugar (especially soft drink), as this can lead to obesity and problems with blood sugar regulation down the track (aka 'diabesity').

- DO share a family evening meal with no distractions at least three times a week (more if possible). And that means no distractions for *anyone* – no phones, no laptops and no TV. Meals should also be civil affairs, so reserve discussions about volatile matters for family meetings or private one-on-one talks.

- DO make it easy for him to choose nutritious snacks. Have baby carrots, cheese sticks, cherry tomatoes, dips and tubs of yoghurt in the fridge and a variety of wholegrain or seeded crackers in the cupboard. Strategically position bowls of fruit on the table. At the very least, teach him how to make popcorn (if he doesn't already know) – it's low cost and high in fibre.

- DO teach him how to cook and prepare food – simple stuff like stirfries, wraps or smoothies. This is a triple win – you save money, he gains skills and he can prepare as much as he wants to eat.

- DO make fibre the key to a filling meal, rather than

more expensive protein options. Stock up on tins of beans and teach him how to use the rice cooker.

EXERCISE

Anyone with a teenage boy who doesn't like sport knows how hard it can be to get them moving. A 2016 paper in the *Journal of Physical Activity and Health* reported that Australian children are among the least active in the world, ranking 21st out of 38 countries, with fewer than 1 in 5 children aged 5–17 meeting the recommended 60 minutes of physical activity each day. Unbelievably, fewer than 1 in 4 students in Year 6 have mastered physical milestones such as catching, throwing, sprinting, jumping and side galloping. This statistic makes sense when you consider that the number of overweight boys has doubled in recent years, with 25 per cent of boys aged 2–17 years now considered overweight or obese.

The rise of Gen XXL is due to many factors:
- Ruthless marketing by fast food giants
- The prevalence of high-calorie, low-nutrient packaged foods in our supermarkets
- A decline in physical activity due to excessive screen time and parental concerns about children 'wandering the neighbourhood'
- Children being driven to and from school
- More erratic family eating habits

The bad news is that overweight or obese children are statistically more likely to be obese teenagers and adults. This is something that we as parents have a say in.

Use technology to encourage exercise

Making exercise interesting, motivating and fun is a good way to start. For younger boys, Zombies, Run! is a mobile 'exergame' for use on both iOS and Android platforms. It became Apple's bestselling health and fitness app within two weeks of its initial release, and has elicited tributes for the way its immersive storyline makes running more fun, and academic attention for its mental health applications. It is based around a mythical place called Abel Township, a small outpost trying to survive the zombie apocalypse. Players act as the character 'Runner 5' through a series of missions during which they walk, jog or run while listening to missions and music through their headphones. Players automatically collect items to build up their base and help the town survive.

There is also a brilliant app called 'Couch to 5K' where your son (or both of you) can progress from minimal exercise to running 5 kilometres (or for 30 minutes) in just nine weeks. It provides a gentle introduction to getting the body moving, starting with alternating between walking and running small distances, and slowly building up to running for 30 minutes non-stop. Once fit, your son can set himself goals and track progress on walking, running, swimming or cycling. The key to success is to ease into the training plan. The beginners' program focuses more on walking and light jogging than running. The app will guide your son through 20–30 minutes of exercise three times a week. It also comes with a fact sheet on stretching called Stay Loose.

There are many other apps and programs out there, as

well as wearable technology like that mentioned in the section about sleep that tracks steps, distance and so on. If your son is interested, encourage him to research the most effective and fun programs with you and try out a few different ones.

Chapter 12
Stress

At its core, stress is the body's response to our thoughts; for example, 'I'm going to fail my exams', 'My girlfriend shouldn't have dumped me', 'I need more money' or 'My parents should be together'. On and on they go, whirring around in our heads, triggering emotions such as sadness, grief, anger or fear, along with physiological responses such as sweating, muscle tension, breathlessness and headaches.

Yet our brain is the most valuable resource we have. It is our meaning-making machine – the organ through which we filter the sensory input from every moment of our lives. We rely on it to be happy, content and emotionally stable as individuals, and to be kind, thoughtful and considerate in our relationships with other people. Yet most of us rarely take the time to look after it – in fact, very few people would even consider that it *needs* looking after. But it does. The rapidly rising rates of depression and anxiety in our society are testament to that. And it is not only adults who are struggling.

Late in 2016, Mission Australia surveyed more than 21 000 young people and asked them to rank how concerned they had been about a number of issues in the past year. The top issue of concern was dealing with stress, with almost half of the respondents indicating that they were either extremely concerned or very concerned about coping with stress.

MINDFULNESS

Many schools are already aware that young people need help to deal with stress and have wellbeing programs in place that teach relaxation techniques such as deep breathing and progressive relaxation. Another brilliant technique is mindfulness meditation, which focuses on being aware of the present moment and noticing feelings and thoughts as they come and go, without getting attached and going down a rabbit hole with them.

My first experience of meditation was at the age of 19. I had just been diagnosed with malignant cancer and been told that I had about eight weeks to live. I was inundated with thoughts and difficult emotions that I did not know how to cope with. Every time I managed to push one down, another would pop up. It was a very stressful time.

I was encouraged to try meditation. I had lots of preconceived ideas about what meditation was; sitting cross-legged, breathing in incense and so on. I thought it would be like taking an aspirin to zap stress. I didn't realise that it could become a preventative method against stress and poor mental health.

As a 19-year-old, meditation taught me to get comfy

with what I was experiencing in the present moment – noticing thoughts and feelings as they arose, and just letting them go. It helped calm my mind. Instead of latching on to negative thoughts and difficult emotions, I allowed them to pass through. They were all stories of the past or the future anyway – nothing to do with me sitting right here, right now. The present moment sounds so ordinary, but it is anything but ordinary.

Use technology to encourage mindfulness

Two Australian apps I recommend for parents and teens are Headspace's Take 10, and Smiling Mind.

Take 10

Take 10 is the free part of the app from Headspace (UK), which teaches the basics of meditation in just 10 minutes a day. If your son likes Take 10, he can access hundreds of hours of meditations, guided and unguided, ranging from 2 to 60 minutes for a monthly, yearly, biannually or 'forever' fee.

Smiling Mind

This Australian app provides unrestricted access to preventative mental health and wellbeing tools based on mindfulness meditation. There are programs for children of different ages as well as programs for adults. The main adult program provides ten modules of mindfulness training and guided meditations (beginning at three minutes in length) for various skills, including:

- staying in the present moment

- listening
- eating mindfully
- paying attention to thoughts and emotions
- following instincts
- practising everyday mindfulness.

Chapter 13

Body image

Body image is usually considered an issue for teenage girls, yet the pressure for boys to conform to particular body types is an increasing problem. While girls are more likely to become anxious and stressed about needing to be thin, boys are more likely to fixate on *gaining* weight in the form of toned and defined muscles. This is known as the Adonis complex. (Adonis was the half man and half god in Greek mythology who was considered the ultimate in masculine beauty to the point that he won the love of Aphrodite, goddess of love and beauty.)

The extent of the problem for young men is largely unknown, though a 2014 study published in *JAMA Pediatrics* found that almost 1 in 5 of the 5500 study participants (aged 12–18) were very concerned about their weight and physique. These concerns mainly centred on being too skinny and lacking muscle tone. A small but significant number (2.5 per cent) were using supplements. Even more worrying, 1 in 3 reported infrequent binge eating, purging or uncontrolled eating. Those who were most concerned about muscularity and thinness were more likely to use drugs, and those who used supplements were more likely to frequently binge drink and use drugs. Previous statistics estimated that the prevalence of eating disorders for males compared to females is as low as 1:10. More recent studies, however, suggest that this ratio is more likely to be 1:4.

MEDIA MATTERS

As with young women, media portrayal has a large role in helping to create obsession with body shape in boys. Advertising in magazines and actors in movies and television increasingly show men with chiselled abs and bulging biceps. For young women, the marketing is about subtracting; for young men, it's about adding. Rather than this being a strange form of gender equality, you can't help feeling that everyone loses.

The proportion of 'undressed' males in advertising has increased since the 1980s, and stories are starting to appear about the size and type of male celebrity bodies; for example, photos of a 'bloated' Leonardo DiCaprio appeared online in 2014 under the heading 'The Great Fatsby'. On Tumblr, there is a page dedicated to 'Fat Male Celebrities', with the catchphrase 'stars packing on the pounds'.

The growing availability of media means that both young men and women are exposed to unrealistic and negative perceptions of undesirable body types 24/7. While the overly muscled bodies of Arnold Schwarzenegger and the like in the 80s stood out for their uniqueness, now images of lean, fit stars like Chris Hemsworth and Justin Bieber are constantly available for comparison. Body shaming is a new sport in the media, evidenced by the popularity of shows such as *The Biggest Loser*.

Online forums such as the Men's Health website and Bodybuilding.com make it easier to seek and share information (whether accurate or not) about diet and fitness. They can be hugely popular; at the time of writing, the forum on supplements on Bodybuilding.com had over 11 million posts, and the forum on teen bodybuilding had over 9 million posts. The danger of some of these forums is that they can branch off into online 'echo chambers'; that is, groups of people so similar that you will only find opinions that agree with yours. When this happens, alternative opinions or points of view are absent for users. Young people can easily become caught up in a world where they not only become more convinced of their own views, but start to adopt more extreme versions. If these sites promote risky training regimes or unattainable body dimensions, this can lead to injury or illness. The situation is not helped by the fact that protein shakes and powders are readily available and unregulated.

Further, some websites or forums may promote the use of steroids. The effects of long-term use of steroids, particularly on adolescent boys who are going through a major period of growth and development, are largely unknown. The availability of online pornography also helps to promote the idea that virile males all have six-packs and chiselled jaw lines.

Little boys are not immune – the body image messages

start young. Measurements of male action figures exceed those of even the biggest bodybuilders. In one 2006 study, researchers compared the physical dimensions of five contemporary action figures (Batman, Superman, GI Joe, the Hulk and Spiderman) to their original counterparts twenty-five years ago. Of seven measures (neck, chest, arm, forearm, waist, thigh and calf), all except for the waist were significantly larger in comparison. The researchers concluded that the increase in action figure dimensions may contribute to an idealised body type that is lean and muscular. Since mainly pre-adolescent boys play with these toys, it's a powerful message to send at a vulnerable developmental age.

ENCOURAGING A HEALTHY BODY IMAGE

The idea here is for parents to help their sons achieve a realistic, healthy body size and shape – not one derived from Hollywood.

- DO model healthy eating and exercise – lots of fresh vegetables, fruits, nuts, seeds, wholegrain foods, animal protein (eggs, dairy and meat) and regular but not obsessive exercise.
- DON'T talk negatively about different body shapes and sizes – aka fat shaming or skinny shaming.
- DO point out that elite athletes, sportspeople and actors have teams of health professionals (including dietitians, trainers, physiotherapists and psychologists) to help them attain their body size and shape.
- DON'T have weight scales in the house. (If you

need them to manage your weight for medical
reasons, keep them in your room.)

- DO discuss what your son is seeing and
  reading online if he shows an interest in weight
  management or bodybuilding. Discuss how forums
  may only provide a certain viewpoint and how
  health is a broader concept.
- DO sit down and talk to your son about what's
  in a protein shake and give him some natural
  options. Nutritionist Catherine Saxelby has some
  good advice on her website about natural sources
  of protein, how much we actually need and what's
  really in protein powder. The additives in some
  brands makes for sobering reading – and while
  there is more protein in many powders than natural
  sources such as eggs or milk, they are considerably
  more expensive and have many more kilojoules.

Chapter 14
Technology

In 2014, Stuart Armstrong, a researcher from the Future of Humanity Institute at the University of Oxford, gained worldwide media coverage when he warned that computers were becoming so clever that they could become our enemies, take all our jobs and eventually 'exterminate' us all. In 2016, physicist Stephen Hawking claimed that it was a 'near certainty' that technology would threaten humanity within the next 1000 to 10000 years.

These warnings are like water off a new iPhone 7 Plus to Prince Boofhead and his contemporaries, who, the research repeatedly shows, are all thoroughly immersed in (and enjoying) technology. In contrast to his parents, who use technology at a comparatively basic level to text or Facebook message friends or hop online to book a holiday, Prince and his peers are extremely tech savvy. Parents are in technological kindergarten compared to their sons.

Today's teenagers have never known a world without computers. They can code, program and are completely up to date with all the latest advances. They are fully conversant with Instagram, Snapchat and the dark web, are comfortable with AI (artificial intelligence) and virtual reality and many have an Amazon Echo that virtually organises their lives for them.

Much of the hysteria about young people, technology and the end of civilisation as we know it is somewhat misplaced. There have been moral panics about young people and the latest gadgets for hundreds of years, be it record players, radio, TV, CDs, mobile phones, social networking or video games. The truth is that while many parents have a penchant for demonising technology, especially the parts that they don't understand, young men love technology. It's not going anywhere – so as parents, we need to get better at understanding, using and supporting our children's positive use of technology.

Unlike many parents, kids see no dividing line between the 'real' world and the 'virtual' world – for them being online *is* the real world. The Australian Communications and Media Authority (ACMA) reports that more than 80 per cent of teenagers aged 12–17 years are regularly online. This is why young people don't necessarily see a difference between online and offline bullying, and why those at risk offline are likely to also be at risk online. In other words, negative use of technology is just a new form of an old problem rather than a product of the technology itself. And the skills that serve your children well in the offline world are also likely (but not always) to be reflected in the online world, such as respect for others, empathy and kindness.

The Pew Research Center in the US found a difference in the ways that teenage boys and girls use technology to socialise. Boys tend to make friends via online gaming, whereas girls are more likely to make friends via social media. According to the study, video games play a critical role in teenage boys' social lives, with more than 80 per cent of boys saying they play video games on a daily or weekly basis – mostly with friends.

SETTING LIMITS ON TECHNOLOGY USE

Unless you are living on the Antarctic shelf (and perhaps even then), conflict about your teenager's use of technology is likely to be a permanent fixture in your home. Many parents can be overzealous in their attempts to control phone, game and computer use due to a lack of confidence or knowledge about the online world. A simple technique for working out if you need to loosen the reins (or tighten them) is to consider if your son's technology use is interfering with his physical and mental wellbeing and his completion of the key tasks of adolescence: making good friends who support him, doing well at school and work, and slowly becoming more independent.

Here are some examples of house rules that you may choose to use or modify for your own circumstances:

- With rights come responsibilities. If your teenager is given a mobile phone, then he must understand and agree to use it in a responsible way – or he doesn't get one.
- Phones must not be used while homework is being completed. He may argue that he needs the

internet to complete his homework; if this is the case, see the next point.

- Teenagers can have privacy in their bedrooms or access to the internet, but they can't have both. The internet is a public place, which means it is used in a 'public' room, such as the lounge room. '
- Older teenagers may be permitted to make phone calls in private, if the phone comes back out with them once the call is completed.
- For younger teenagers, their use of technology should be conditional on the premise that they will show you, whenever asked, what they are doing online.
- Set clear time limits on the use of technology for leisure. For example, primary school children can be allowed one hour per day of screen entertainment. This can increase to two hours in secondary school.
- Set a time at night when all devices are put on charge or locked away in a public room of the house.
- Switch off the wi-fi overnight.

For younger teenagers, you may wish to use one of the tools available to enforce the boundaries that you set. Free software programs such as Our Pact, Cold Turkey and Self Control are all easy to use and allow you to block, for a set time, websites that your son may be distracted by when he should be concentrating on other tasks, such as homework or chores.

For older adolescents, don't rely on filters – maintain

a watchful eye on their technology use. Smart kids can work around filters in a flash.

Encourage and initiate outdoor or other indoor activities, with offline friends and family. But be aware that the friends your son has online are important to him and may help him feel valued and supported. Some young people benefit greatly from the support offered to them by the online community, especially if they are experiencing issues that might mark them as 'different' in the real world, such as having a disability or chronic illness.

Chapter 15

Gaming

When you think about video games, it's not hard to conjure up an image of a pale, unwashed 15-year-old boy sitting alone in his dark bedroom surrounded by soft-drink cans and junk-food wrappers. Yet the Digital Australia 2016 report shows that this impression is far from accurate. Video games are widely played in Australia by people of all ages, and around half of players are now female. The average age of gamers is 33, and there are many different genres and styles of play, including first person shooters, platform games, role-playing games and real-time or turn-based strategy games. Plus, you can play them on a smartphone, laptop, computer or gaming console.

TALK TO YOUR SON ABOUT GAMING

It's worth understanding that video games are vital for many boys to engage with their peers and friends, more so than for girls. US research by the Pew Research Center shows that this makes boys feel more connected to friends. So it's not necessarily all negative.

Needless to say, the best way to find out what he is doing online is to strike up a conversation with him (see page 65 for tips on communicating with boys). Here are some questions to guide the conversation:

- What kinds of games do you like playing? What do you like about these games? What's your favourite?
- What's your greatest achievement in a game?
- How do you feel when you are gaming? How do you feel when you stop?
- Do you like playing on your own, or games with other people?
- If you play with other people, do you know these people offline? How important are these friends to you? Can you talk to them about difficult things?
- Do you play when you should be doing something else, e.g. sleeping or doing homework?
- Is it hard to stop? Do you feel sometimes like you have to play, even when it's not all that much fun?

If your son answers yes to the last two points, it could be an indication that gaming is interfering with his well-being. See the end of this chapter for advice on signs to look for and how to respond.

THE BENEFITS OF GAMING

The nature of video games has changed substantially over the past few years. Games are becoming more complex, realistic and social, and require engagement on many levels. In the past, much research has focused on finding evidence for the negative effects of gaming. Yet the evidence suggests that poor wellbeing is likely to be a cause rather than an effect of unhealthy levels of gaming. If we can find ways of engaging these young people in game play that is designed to increase their psychosocial wellbeing, then technology may become part of the solution, rather than the problem.

A 2014 article in the journal *American Psychologist* suggested that video games may benefit young people's psychological health in several areas:

- Cognitive benefits – benefits include improved spatial skills, hand–eye coordination, problem-solving and creativity.
- Motivational benefits – the constant feedback in video games rewards persistence, which is a skill that can transfer to work and school contexts.
- Emotional benefits – real-life simulations allow players to experience both positive and negative emotions and to learn to regulate them. Other research associates video game play with relaxation and stress reduction. They may play a role in providing space for young people to let off steam or escape problems for a while.
- Social benefits – US research indicates that around three-quarters of gamers play with friends, and that those who link up with other players are less likely to have social problems than those who play alone. Many multiplayer games require a mixture of cooperation and competition, so the level of pro-social versus antisocial behaviour of players and their avatars depends on how the game is played,

not the subject matter or content of the game.

Charlie was starting at a different high school to many
of the boys with whom he attended primary school.
He was naturally quite an anxious boy and was worried
that he would have trouble making new friends. At
the Year 7 orientation day he met some boys who were
going to be in his class and they exchanged mobile
phone numbers. Over the summer holidays Charlie
messaged his classmates and played online games with
them. When he turned up for his first day of high
school, he couldn't wait to get into class to talk to his
new friends.

SHOULD I PLAY GAMES WITH HIM?

Many boys long for an opportunity to have an adult
engage in a video game with them – and this may be
a good idea. A study from Arizona State University in
2013 looked at intergenerational play using commercial,
off-the-shelf video games. In a series of focus groups,
researchers Elisabeth Hayes and Sinem Siyahhan found
that many parents don't understand that video games
are often tailored for sharing and include lessons in
science, literacy and problem-solving. They also open up
the possibility for 'teachable moments'; in other words,
naturally occurring opportunities to engage your son in
conversations about things that matter. The other benefit
is the opportunity for the child to be the teacher once in a
while – teaching parents about game play. The researchers

found that these sharing experiences cultivated family bonding, learning and wellbeing, and concluded that parents 'miss a huge opportunity when they walk away from playing video games with their kids'.

The university's Center for Games and Impact has created a number of 'impact guides' (https://gamesand impact.org/impact-guides/) that provide parents and players with tools to understand the game and inspire thinking about what the game offers in terms of building a knowledgeable and empathetic citizenship.

DOES PLAYING VIOLENT VIDEO GAMES LEAD TO REAL-LIFE VIOLENCE?

Games such as *Call of Duty*, *Assassin's Creed*, *Grand Theft Auto* and *World of Warcraft* are all popular with teenage boys and all involve violence. Yet a report by the American Psychological Association, which reviewed all the research between 2009 and 2013, found that violent video games are unlikely to exacerbate aggressive behaviour in boys unless they have previously demonstrated violent or aggressive behaviour (see chapter 20 for more about adolescent violence in the home).

IS HE GAMING TOO MUCH?

It depends. As I mentioned in the previous chapter, screen entertainment is okay as long as it does not interfere with your son's ability to negotiate the developmental tasks of adolescence. If he also has offline friends, is handling his schoolwork and homework, and is generally becoming a more responsible and independent human being, the existing evidence suggests that low to moderate use of video games may in fact have some benefits. Other factors are far more influential in whether a child or young person experiences wellbeing, such as family functioning and parent–child communication.

If you are worried about the amount of time your son is spending playing games, consider the following questions:

- Why is he spending so much time playing games? Is there something else going on in your son's life that he would rather avoid? If you are not sure, just ask him – preferably not while he is playing. (See page 65 for tips on talking to teenage boys.)
- Is the game single player or multiplayer? If it's multiplayer, is he able to take a break, or does the game require him and his 'team' to continue to play in order to avoid defeat? Are there other team members relying on him? If so, peer pressure to maintain game play can cause stress or distress if your son is not confident enough to leave the game without incurring the wrath of his peers.

Here are some signs that he may need help:
- He craves more game time.
- He suffers from chronic dry eyes or migraines.
- He neglects personal hygiene.
- He lies about how much he is playing or denies that the amount of time he plays is too much.
- He has no friends in the offline world.
- He refuses to leave the house for fear of missing out

on something in the game.
- He is irritable or snappy if he's not at the computer.

Tell your son you are worried and show him this list of symptoms. If he argues with you on every one or flat-out denies them, then it is important for you to step up and help him reduce the amount of time he is spending on gaming. Limit playing time to a certain number of days per week, and encourage him to follow other pursuits in the time he now has free. Also encourage him to see a mental health professional (see chapter 24).

Chapter 16

Online gambling

It's impossible to talk about online gaming without addressing online gambling, due to the increasingly blurred lines between the two. Many online games have gambling characteristics (e.g. *Candy Crush*) or are a soft introduction to poker games and casino style games (e.g. *Heart of Vegas*).

The Australian Gambling Research Centre reports that people who play simulated gambling games are more likely to report gambling problems and engage in commercial gambling. The concern expressed by the researchers is that, along with advertising, it is possible that gambling is being normalised and portrayed as harmless. Yet it's not – Australians spend nearly $20 billion per year on gambling, mostly on poker machines. In 2014, adults lost on average almost $1300 per year in Australia – double the amount lost in the US and New Zealand and 2.5 times more than in the UK. Gambling leads to damaged family relationships, financial difficulties and mental health problems, and it is associated with family violence. It's definitely not harmless fun.

As we saw in the previous chapter, young men are more likely to play video games than young women, but they are also at greater risk of developing a gambling problem. This may be due in part to the increasing prevalence of sports betting, but other risk factors include having a parent or a sibling with a gambling problem. If Dad is putting a couple of bucks on your favourite horse for you each week, it starts to normalise the behaviour. Combine this with the gambling characteristics of online games and it's a problem waiting to happen.

Tristan was a successful young professional who wasn't all that interested in online games and sports betting until he broke his ankle playing footy. He was laid up for so long he started to get bored – he was used to being super active and sitting around really wasn't his thing. A mate suggested a site called Moneygames, which was a fantasy sports platform where members paid to play in contests either with friends or other members of the Moneygames community. Tristan could choose his ultimate fantasy team, pay an entry fee and watch as his players accumulated points. When he won the prize pool in his second week, he felt he really had it nailed. There were so many contests to choose from and they were so easy to enter! Yet, even though each contest only had a minimum $2 entry fee, he was soon playing ten contests at a time and increasing his bets until eventually he was betting hundreds of dollars on Russian ice hockey games. It was only when, one day, he calculated he had spent around $10 000 on online gambling that he realised he had to get some help.

The Victorian Responsible Gambling Foundation (VRGF) has compiled a list of behaviours that may suggest your son is developing an addiction to gambling:

- Obsessively playing simulated gambling apps and games to the point that it interferes with eating, sleeping, personal hygiene and/or attending school or work.
- Spending more time online with gambling apps and games and less time with friends or doing activities that he usually enjoys.
- Talking a lot about betting or focusing on the betting aspects of a sports game.
- Borrowing or asking for money from family and friends when he is known to be playing gambling apps or betting.

It is important to note that, like other addictive behaviours, gambling is often a sign that there are under-lying emotional problems not being addressed. Research conducted by Monash University, the University of Melbourne and the Victorian government in 2008 found that more than 70 per cent of problem gamblers were at risk of depression and more than one-third had a severe mental disorder. While it is difficult to know whether gambling leads to mental health problems or vice versa, it's clear that the link needs to be better understood. It may also mean that preventative approaches targeting a gambler's rational choices (e.g. 'gamble responsibly') are less likely to be effective when underlying mental health problems exist.

The best way to approach the problem is to talk to your son about what you have observed. The VRGF has some great tips as well as a guide for talking to teens about gambling (see www.responsiblegambling.vic.gov.au).

You can also call the Gambler's Help Youthline on 1800 262 376. It's a free and confidential helpline open 24/7 for young people who are worried about their own or someone else's gambling behaviour, or for parents who are worried about their young person's gambling behaviour.

Chapter 17
Sex

Australian author Joanne Fedler nicely sums up sexual development in the teenage years as being 'between intimacies' – the intimacy of a parent–child relationship in the early years and an intimate partner relationship in the late teenage/early adult years. And as these intimacies trade places, much experimentation and many new behaviours will take place. According to the 2013 National Survey of Australian Secondary Students and Sexual Health, around 25 per cent of teenagers had had sexual intercourse by Year 10 and 50 per cent by Year 12. In addition, 1 in 8 young men reported that their most recent sexual encounter was with someone of the same sex.

For young teenage boys, puberty heralds the ability to reproduce, and wet dreams and involuntary erections may become common events. Ideally, it would be great if dads had conversations about these events (since women cannot speak from experience). Yet the sexual health study I mentioned earlier found that mothers tend to be the most common source of information about sex and relationships. In any case, your son will appreciate reassurance that nocturnal emissions are common and nothing to be ashamed about. Equally, he may appreciate knowing that while erections may pop up at the least convenient and most embarrassing times and often can't be controlled, over time this will become less frequent. And if his mates laugh at him, they should remember that it's likely to happen to them, too.

TALKING TO TEENAGE BOYS ABOUT SEX

- Don't wait for the 'right moment' – initiate conversations about sex as part of everyday life, e.g. while in the car, cleaning the house, shopping – sex education should be an ongoing conversation, not a one-off.
- Use teachable moments – if sex comes up in a television show, movie, YouTube clip or music video, use it as a starting point for discussion.
- Acknowledge that sex can be a difficult or uncomfortable subject, but explain that it's important to keep talking.
- If you don't know the answer to a question, it's okay to be honest about it. You can suggest looking it up together.
- Be direct. Clearly state your feelings about specific issues, such as consent and pornography.
- Present the risks objectively, such as sexually transmitted infections and unplanned pregnancies.
- Explain that oral sex isn't a risk-free alternative to intercourse.

- Don't finger-wag or try to scare him into avoiding sexual activity.
- Listen carefully and be aware of his pressures, challenges and concerns.
- Reward questions by saying, 'I'm glad you chatted to me.'
- And most importantly of all, discuss consent and clearly explain that no means no.

PORNOGRAPHY

Teenagers' access to pornography is now simple, free and pretty much routine – it takes two clicks of a mouse to access the type of pornography that was once only available in the R-rated section of the video shop. This is highly unlikely to change – our only option is to give our teenagers the skills and knowledge to navigate this world and to present alternative narratives about love, sex and relationships. Don't rely on school to do this job – parents (and other older family members) need to step up and be much-needed sources of information.

It's likely to come as no great surprise that the most frequent underage users of online pornography are teenage boys, but girls are also accessing or unintentionally viewing porn. One study of young people aged 11–16 years by Middlesex University in 2016 showed that by 15 years of age, around two-thirds of children had viewed pornography, with more boys viewing online pornography by choice than girls. Almost half of the boys surveyed wanted to try out what they had seen, compared to 29 per cent of the girls. It was equally likely that a child would stumble across pornography as search deliberately for it. So if you feel safe in the knowledge that your son is not the type of boy to look at pornography, it's unlikely to matter because he'll probably see it anyway.

As parents, we must acknowledge and engage in discussions about how online pornography is affecting relationships between young men and women. The Australian website itstimewetalked.com.au has a number of fact sheets for parents, including how you can start the 'porn talk'. Here are some tips:

- Think through beforehand what you want to ask and say, and how to make the conversation private. A car trip is always a good option – your son doesn't need to make eye contact but nor can he get away easily.
- A request from your son for the latest technology is a great opportunity for a parent to initiate a discussion about risks, benefits and expectations of technology use, including pornography, sexting and cyber safety.
- Use newspaper articles, billboards or films to discuss gender stereotypes or sexualised imagery.
- If a talk doesn't go well, don't worry. It's an ongoing conversation that can come up again at different ages and different times.
- If you discover that your child has accessed pornography, stay calm. Spend some time thinking about the situation before acting. Your son will learn from not just your words but your whole response.

Talking to your son about porn

Here are some key messages to impart when talking to your son about porn.

1. Pornography is not reality. Most people in online pornography are acting – they're performing for the viewer. The bodies of many pornography performers – like those of models and sports stars – do not reflect how most people look.

2. Porn sex is not safe sex. Porn often shows people doing all sorts of unsafe things, such as oral sex directly following anal sex, or ejaculation in mouths and eyes. The reality is that these behaviours can spread STIs and HIV.

3. Porn distorts pleasure. Porn focuses on particular types of sexual behaviours that do not reflect what most people – particularly women – like or want in real life.

4. Sex is not just for guys to enjoy. The vast majority of porn consumers are men, so porn focuses on guys getting what they want. The women are often there to please the men – and they may be treated terribly in the process.

5. Women are not sex objects. Women's sexuality is used to sell all sorts of things – from cars to body moisturiser to alcohol. Porn takes it one step further. Porn says that women are just objects for guys' sexual pleasure.

6. Porn commonly depicts – and strengthens – racial and gender stereotypes.

7. Consent is crucial to good sex. If you watch porn,

you might think that everyone wants to have sex all the time, and consent is implied. But they don't and it may not be.

8. Sex can have meaning. Porn communicates that sex doesn't require intimacy, love or affection – it's just something people do with anyone.

Research is in its early days, but it's likely that the effects of frequent and routine viewing of pornography can contribute to harmful gender stereotypes, unhealthy views of women and acceptance of violence towards women. Common acts in online pornography include gagging, choking and slapping, almost universally directed at women, alongside general themes of women's degradation and humiliation. As a masterclass in under-statement – online pornography has certainly changed the landscape of sexual development.

Chapter 18
Alcohol

When you ask parents what drug they are most concerned about when their sons hit high school, it is not uncommon for them to reel off a list that includes methamphetamines (such as ice), cannabis or even cocaine. Rarely do they mention alcohol. Yet, alcohol causes more deaths, injury and illness among young people than any other drug. Every week in Victoria, for example:

- around 30 young people are assaulted in incidents involving alcohol
- around 25 young people are admitted to hospital because of alcohol
- more than 10 young people are seriously injured in alcohol-related road crashes.

But there is some good news. According to the 2013 National Drug Strategy Household Survey, the proportion of teens aged 12–17 who had *not* had an alcoholic drink in the previous 12 months rose from 64 per cent in 2010 to 72 per cent in 2013. This means that for almost three-quarters of young people in this age group, alcohol use is a non-issue. Young people are also continuing to delay having their first drink, with first-time alcohol use increasing from 14.4 years in 1998 to 15.7 years in 2013.

Yet, despite the considerable successes of the public health movement, there remains a stubborn, hard-to-reach minority of Australian males who seem to think that alcohol should be one of the basic food groups. For these young men (aged in their late teens and twenties) it is inconceivable that one could go out and not drink, and drinking to excess is a way of proving one's masculinity. For them it would be normal to consume 15–20 standard drinks on a 'drinking night' and less than ten drinks would be considered a quiet night. These quantities place them at serious risk of an alcohol-related injury and of alcohol-related harm over their lifetime.

ALCOHOL'S EFFECTS ON THE DEVELOPING BRAIN

While you might be cheered by the fact that fewer teenagers are drinking alcohol, the fact remains that a young person's brain is still under construction until the mid-twenties (possibly later for young men). The body of research about the effects of alcohol on the developing brain is still embryonic, but there seems to be a growing consensus that the younger a person starts drinking alcohol, the more damage it will do. And unfortunately, the 2013 National Drug Strategy Household Survey found that around 1 in 10 teenagers aged 12–17 were having more than four standard drinks at least once a month.

This is unacceptable, especially when you consider what alcohol does to the brain.

Alcohol affects the hippocampus, which is responsible for memory and learning. Professor Dan Lubman and his colleagues published a study that found that heavy and extended alcohol use is associated with a 10 per cent reduction in the size of the hippocampus. The research also demonstrated that the function of the hippocampus is particularly sensitive to alcohol because of its toxic effect on the nerve cells of the hippocampus, causing them to be damaged or destroyed.

Another part of the brain sensitive to alcohol is the prefrontal cortex. As we saw in chapter 3, this is the part of the brain responsible for language, planning, making judgements and decisions and controlling impulses, which undergoes the greatest transformation during adolescence. Research shows that teens who drink heavily have a smaller prefrontal cortex than young people of the same age who do not drink. The key message here is that alcohol use needs to be delayed until children are at least 18, in line with the recommendations from the National Health and Medical Research Council.

WHY TEENS DRINK

Why, then, do so many young men indulge in risky drinking? Social scientists have blamed poor regulation of alcohol advertising, growing up in disconnected communities amidst unprecedented social change, global economic turmoil, high levels of family breakdown, stratospheric levels of discretionary income, and the 'tamagotchi' parenting practices I have outlined of zero supervision, no limits or boundaries, and an epidemic culture of 'I-just-want-to-be-his-friend' indulgence. In fact, almost 40 per cent of underage drinkers say they get their supply of alcohol from their parents. This is in spite of the fact that most states already have 'secondary supply' legislation, which makes it illegal to sell or supply alcohol to people under the age of 18 years, and hefty fines for those who allow other people's kids to drink in their home against the wishes of their parents. Which brings me to my next point – if you want your son to drink responsibly, be a role model.

> Our son is 16 and desperately wants to have a party at our home. We are fortunate enough to have a large backyard and a pool, which would make it a pleasant venue for the celebration. However, he is pressuring us to provide alcohol and says he will be a laughing stock if we don't provide any. He says all we need to do is ensure that each of his friends brings along a note signed by their parents saying they are allowed to be served alcohol. I have heard many different stories about this and am totally confused. What should I do?

The legal age for drinking in Australia is 18 and, as outlined in this chapter, there is not a single argument that could possibly support the use of alcohol any earlier than this. In spite of this, a culture is developing in Australia that sees parents providing alcohol at parties in increasing amounts as their child gets closer to 18 years of age. Secondary supply laws, which refer to the supply of alcohol to anyone under the age of 18, vary across the country. Parents and other adults need to be aware of these laws, particularly as they apply to common events in adolescence such as teenage parties in the family home or sleepovers at friends' places.

The best source of up-to-date information can be found on the DrinkWise website (www.drinkwise.org.au).

TIPS TO DELAY DRINKING

There's no denying that alcohol use is central to Australian culture yet, as we have seen, it is important to support young people to avoid alcohol for as long as possible, particularly before they turn 18. The following tips may help.

Keep him busy

While this suggestion seems to be straight out of the university of the bleeding obvious, children whose parents encourage engagement in hobbies, exercise, sport and schoolwork are less likely to use alcohol. In other words, while young men are engaged in doing challenging activities that build resilience, they are less likely to need to take unhealthy risks like binge drinking alcohol.

Model responsible alcohol use

One of the most significant risk factors for problem drinking among young people is having parents who drink. This increases both the chance that your son will engage in alcohol use and the risk for more significant alcohol-related problems. Research from the University of Melbourne shows that the earlier a child is exposed to alcohol at home, the greater the likelihood that he will initiate early alcohol use and engage in problem drinking.

At this point you may be comforting yourself with the thought that you drink moderately and responsibly, so you have nothing to worry about. Unfortunately, studies show that even moderate parental drinking is also associated with undesirable adolescent outcomes. For example, data from the Mater-University of Queensland birth cohort study demonstrated that maternal alcohol consumption of one or more drinks every day (assessed when the offspring were aged 14) was a strong predictor of alcohol use disorder in children at age 21, even after controlling for a range of biological, familial and interpersonal factors. So while we can't discount the impact of genetic loading or the impact of the environment − both of which can contribute to such problems − we also can't ignore the role of social learning as an important contributing factor.

Get to know his mates

A truism in the whole teenage drinking debate is that there are three great influencers: parents, promotion (marketing) and peers. It is the peer factor that is often the most difficult to control. The risk of binge drinking is exponentially higher if your teenager associates with peers who binge drink. Who your son hangs out with is critical.

By spending time with your son and his peers, which is hopefully a natural extension of the early years, not only do you get to assess the character of those peers but inevitably will come into contact with their parents. This allows you to suss out the family's values, attitudes and beliefs around alcohol, other drugs and supervision, all of which are important if their children become close friends with your own.

Encourage critical thinking

Our sons are bombarded with many different messages about alcohol as they grow up, particularly from the alcohol industry. In social media, the industry has cleverly circumvented many of the restrictions that usually exist around alcohol advertising and promotion and have deliberately associated their product with sport. This means their products are inevitably marketed directly to young men, despite the fact that it is technically illegal for many of them to purchase the product.

Give him the facts

Your 15-year-old son is unlikely to be the least bit interested in how the brain is affected by alcohol, largely because at this age he's not able to envisage future consequences of his current behaviour. However, it is essential to have an open, frank and honest dialogue with your son about alcohol. He needs to know that young people who start drinking early, drink a lot or drink often are more likely to hurt or injure themselves, take part in risky sexual activity, suffer from a range of cancers, develop substance abuse and alcohol addictions, experience mental health problems, and damage their brains, livers and kidneys forever.

For tips on discussing the effects of alcohol in a

rational, credible (non-fearmongering way) have a look at theothertalk.org.au. It's also great for parents who want more information on alcohol and other drugs and ways to protect their children from associated harms. See the Resources section at the end of this book for other websites that may help.

WHAT IF HE COMES HOME DRUNK?

What if you have tried your best to prevent your high-school-aged son from drinking and he comes home smashed?

- First, don't panic! Ensure his physical safety and help him recover. Sobering up will take time (around one standard drink per hour) and none of the conventional myths will help – not black coffee, cold showers or bacon and egg rolls.
- Don't engage him in conversation while he is still drunk – wait until he has sobered up, and then get the facts.
- Make it clear that you don't approve of underage drinking, and implement consequences.
- Avoid moralising – preaching and trying to control your son's behaviour may well inspire rebellion rather than agreement (especially if you drink yourself).
- Talk to him about ways to deal with peer pressure. Use examples from your own experience.
- Keep the lines of communication open so that you always know where he is, what he is doing and with whom he is doing it.

Joshua's drinking began at school. He was part of a group in Year 9 who seemed to contract a teen binge drinking virus. He would go to parties most weekends, sleeping over at different friends' houses so that his parents would not realise he was regularly getting hammered. His parents drank a glass of wine with their meals most evenings, but comforted themselves with the knowledge that they had never been drunk in front of Joshua.

It wasn't until Joshua turned 18, and the family celebrated his birthday at a local restaurant with a large group of friends and extended family, that they realised their son had a problem with alcohol.

WARNING SIGNS OF A DRINKING PROBLEM

If you know that your son is drinking, it is important to recognise the signs of a drinking problem. Early intervention, in the form of prompt expert assessment and treatment, is associated with better outcomes.

Here are some warning signs of alcohol dependence:
- He wants to drink alcohol on his own.
- He is constantly trying to organise the opportunity for his next drink.
- He needs increasing amounts of alcohol to get drunk.
- His friends are worried about the amount he drinks.
- He has blacked out or forgotten what he did when he was drinking.
- He drinks more than he intends to, or can't stop when he wants to.

- He avoids responsibilities, such as work or study, due to drinking or hangovers.
- He says he needs a drink to feel 'normal' (though he might use the words 'to relax' or 'feel okay').

Chapter 19
Other drugs

According to the 2013 Australian National Drug Strategy Household Survey, alcohol, cannabis and tobacco are the three most commonly used drugs among people aged 12–17. Around 10 per cent had more than four standard drinks at least once a month; around 15 per cent had tried cannabis and just under 4 per cent smoked cigarettes on a daily basis.

An earlier (2011) study of Australian secondary school students' use of tobacco, alcohol and over-the-counter and illicit substances found that:

- 3 per cent had tried amphetamines
- 3 per cent had tried ecstasy (MDMA)
- 20 per cent had deliberately sniffed inhalants, such as petrol, glue or solvents, at least once
- 1.7 per cent had used cocaine
- 1.6 per cent had tried heroin.

The same report also found that around 4–5 per cent of students aged 13–18 had used tranquillisers in the past month. Of those who had used them in the past year, parents were their main source. This is disturbing when you consider the fact that in 2016 almost twice as many overdose deaths were linked to legal prescription medication as to illegal drugs.

WHY TEENS USE DRUGS

When asked why they started smoking cannabis, most teenagers will say it was because their friends did, and that they wanted to be accepted by the rest of the group. This is the old peer pressure excuse, to which most parents may rightly reply, 'So if your mates jumped off a three-storey building, would you do that too?'

Almost every school cohort can boast a group of disaffected, disaffiliated, sensation-seeking young men who are likely to experiment with drugs or even engage in other risk-taking behaviours such as property damage or shoplifting. Such groups exist due to a combination of lax parenting, a particular type of personality and temperament, and the difficulties as a result of family circumstances. Being raised in fractured, broken or blended families; poverty; mental illness; poor academic or sporting achievement; and having a parent who uses drugs are all risk factors for young people in developing an early dependency on cannabis, alcohol or other drugs.

TIPS TO PREVENT DRUG TAKING

Are there any foolproof, 100-per-cent guaranteed methods for preventing your son from ever experimenting with drugs? The answer is a definite no, short of nailing him to the floor, chaining him to the bed or locking him in his bedroom (all currently illegal). The moment you have a child, he is at risk. But, as explained in the alcohol chapter, there are some techniques that can substantially reduce the likelihood of a young person experimenting with drugs.

Talk to him

Having a communicative and trusting relationship with your son is crucial. A strong connection means you are able to set limits on his behaviour without destroying that relationship.

Share your thoughts, feelings, attitudes and beliefs and clearly articulate the family rules about what is acceptable behaviour regarding the use of illicit drugs.

Talk to your son about the dangers of drug use, drawing on teachable moments from the media (e.g. when there is an overdose at a music festival). But avoid preaching, exaggeration or finger-wagging. It's best to frame it as an open and honest discussion about drugs.

It is beyond the scope of this book to describe each of the illegal drugs your son is likely to encounter, but there are excellent resources available online to help you communicate and negotiate about and understand drug use in adolescents (see page 189).

Get to know his mates

One of the greatest predictors of your son using drugs is him having friends who use. This is why it is so important to monitor where your son is and with whom. As I've said elsewhere in the book, invite his friends over – feed them, talk to them and, if possible, meet their parents.

Be a role model

First, I would encourage parents to practise what they preach. Not surprisingly, it's less likely that your son will abstain from illicit drug use if you or your partner come home from work and light up a spliff on the back porch. In my experience, even parents who attempt to hide their own drug use (e.g. by smoking a joint after their son has gone to bed) will always be found out.

Second, model healthy attitudes to diet, sleep and exercise, as these provide the groundwork for overall wellbeing.

Finally, if you can manage your emotions and resist peer pressure, you provide an excellent example of how your son can manage his own emotions without resorting to drugs or alcohol.

Keep him busy

Supporting and encouraging pro-social activities such as sport, art, music, dance and drama means your son will be able to test his skills and abilities in a safe arena. Being involved in the community (e.g. through a cultural, religious or political event or program) is another way for young people to develop skills and build resilience.

SIGNS HE MAY BE USING DRUGS

Parents who do not adequately supervise and monitor their offspring are more likely to be blindsided by the revelation that their sons are regularly using drugs. In addition, some of the behaviours associated with drug use are very similar to those of your average teenager, so it can be challenging to tell the difference. However, there are some specific signs or behaviours that may suggest your son is experimenting with drugs. If your garden hose keeps getting shorter and soft-drink bottles disappear, for example, this may be a clue that your son is smoking bongs. More subtle signs include the following:

- A decline in academic performance
- A sudden and aggressive protection of privacy
- A change in peer group
- Weight loss
- Poor hygiene
- Fatigue and mood swings

Jenny and Brian had always been a bit concerned about Malcolm's struggle to find solid friendships at primary school. High school wasn't any easier, even though Jenny did her best to encourage him to do sport, music or any extracurricular activity he wanted. Malcolm, however, preferred to play computer games, like his mostly unemployed father, and would do so every chance he got.

Malcolm coped well academically, managing distinctions in most subjects despite rushing to complete all of his schoolwork during class time. But he hated school and both parents often had trouble getting him to attend.

Towards the end of Year 10, Malcolm began socialising with a new boy who had moved from another school and they began skateboarding together. Jenny and Brian were thrilled. Not only did Malcolm have a friend, but he was getting out of the house, was exercising and seemed animated and happy.

In the early months of Year 11, Malcolm (for whom puberty was quite late) had a considerable growth spurt. At the same time his friendship circle widened to include a crew of skaters from several schools. His grades had begun to slip but Jenny and Brian put it down to the pressure of doing VCE subjects. Malcolm also began skipping classes every couple of weeks (although he always had an excuse) and was staying over at his mates' houses most weekends. He seemed angry and tired when he was home, and anxious to see his friends. Jenny thought this was normal adolescent behaviour, along with his filthy room, reluctance to shower and his loose, baggy clothing with a hoodie constantly covering his face.

Then one morning, when Jenny was trying to get him up to go to school, she saw his emaciated frame under the blankets and realised that something was very wrong. She took him to their local GP, where, to her horror, she soon learned that her son had been using every cent they gave him to buy alcohol, cigarettes, cannabis and hallucinogenic drugs for himself and the other members of his group. This marked the beginning of a long, slow journey to recovery, involving a dietitian and individual and family therapy.

WHAT TO DO IF HE'S USING DRUGS

- DO resist the temptation to become hysterical. Take a deep breath, pour yourself some calming chamomile tea and get control of your emotions before you confront him. Resist the urge to call the police, raid his room or conduct a strip search.
- DO conduct your own research (see page 189).
- DO raise the issue directly with your son when he comes home. State what has been found (or found out) and why you are concerned, in as calm a manner as possible. Again, resist the temptation to scream and yell as this will only trigger defensiveness and shut down the very communication you are trying to keep open.
- DON'T use ultimatums, as they will only push him into a corner. Try to educate him on health and lifestyle risks.
- DON'T allow your son to avoid any consequences that arise from his behaviour while using or dealing with drugs.

Seventeen-year-old Stephen's parents were shocked when his father received a phone call from the police. While they were aware that Stephen had dabbled in illicit drugs, and they had unsuccessfully tried to deal with the issue, they had no idea that he had tried his hand at dealing in the park near his school. Stephen's parents supported him when he had to make a court appearance, and paid his fines the moment they were

issued. When he ended up at the police station for
the same offence three weeks after the first time, his
parents were devastated. They did not know what else
to do.

The problem here is that Stephen was denied the
opportunity to learn from the consequences of his
behaviour. As painful and difficult as it can be for parents
to watch their son's behaviour spiral, Stephen's behaviour
is unlikely to improve if they keep protecting him from
those consequences.

Chapter 20
Adolescent violence in the home

Adolescent violence is a poorly understood and under-researched form of family violence. It refers to any act by a young person that intends to cause physical, psychological or financial damage to a parent or carer. We don't really know how often it happens, but many family services are reporting an increase in the number of families they see experiencing this problem.

One small study in the western suburbs of Sydney discovered that a staggering 70 per cent of mothers reported physical violence, intimidation or financial abuse from their teenage children. Often parents will be reluctant to disclose the violence due to guilt or fear of the consequences. The bottom line is that this sort of violence is likely to be more common than we think, but massively underreported.

Overseas studies give us some further insight into the problem. A 2011 US review by Routt and Anderson estimated that adolescent violence occurs in around 1 in 10 families, a ratio that increases to 1 in 3 in single-parent families.

A 2010 UK study revealed that over a one-year period, almost 1900 incidents of adolescent violence, threats of violence or criminal damage were reported to police from homes in the Greater London area. Offenders were overwhelmingly male (87 per cent) and victims were substantially more likely to be female (78 per cent). Two-thirds of the cases involved a son–mother relationship, with a further one-fifth involving a son–father relationship.

Mothers are more likely to be the victims of adolescent abuse because:

- they are more likely to interact with the child
- they are more likely to head single-parent homes
- fathers may defend themselves more readily and effectively.

However, fathers, siblings and other family members also experience physical or verbal abuse from young people.

WHAT CAUSES ADOLESCENT VIOLENCE?

A University of Oxford study between 2010 and 2013 found no single explanation for why adolescent violence occurs in the home. Indeed, the cause is often a mystery to parents who have other children who don't engage in such behaviours. The abuse may escalate and form a pattern over time. Physical assault of a parent or other family member may occur, along with smashing property, kicking holes in doors, breaking windows, throwing things at parents and making threats.

Adolescent violence occurs in homes in both rich and

poor suburbs and, while there is no single explanation for it, there are certain common factors:

- Having weak emotional bonds with parents
- Exercising authority in family matters
- Being so accustomed to getting what they want that they don't know how to cope when they don't
- Having a sense of entitlement for material goods, money or privileges such as being driven around
- Not experiencing boundaries in childhood
- Hitting their parents if they didn't get what they wanted when they were younger
- Learning early in childhood that escalating to anger and fury will result in their demands being met
- Witnessing family violence or abuse as a way of solving problems
- Experiencing harsh, authoritarian parenting
- Having mental health and/or drug problems
- Displaying a lack of empathy for victims

Amanda couldn't quite believe it when Max came home and said he'd lost his phone. It was the third time in two months. She knew that she needed to take a stand about Max's carelessness, although there was always a risk that it would set him off. So when he asked for a new phone (not just a phone, but the latest and newest iPhone at a mere $1399) she said she thought that Max could contribute somehow, like maybe mowing the lawn once a week. He looked at her incredulously before leaning in close to her and screaming in her face, 'Unbelievable! What do you expect from me! I can't exactly NOT have a phone!' Amanda's shoulders tensed and she could feel her heart start to hammer. She went to say something to appease the situation, but before she could open her mouth Max picked up her own phone and threw it out the kitchen window. He stormed up the stairs, and the last words Amanda heard were, 'I may as well just kill myself for all anyone cares.'

COPING WITH A VIOLENT ADOLESCENT

Some parents may find it difficult to differentiate adolescent violence from the 'acting out' that some adolescents engage in from time to time. The difference is the abuse of power. A violent adolescent will try to dominate, coerce and control his parents or others.

Violence or abuse is never, ever acceptable. Letting it go, making excuses or minimising it is NOT okay. It needs to be addressed not only to ensure the safety of the family, but also so that it doesn't lead to intergenerational use of violence to solve problems. The boy who gets the green light at home could be the teenager who lands the coward's punch at the pub a few years later.

Here are some strategies for coping with a violent adolescent:

- Never put up with intimidating or violent behaviour, even if it seems trivial or insignificant.
- If your son is getting angry, communicate with him in a level, even tone. His brain isn't fully formed yet, but yours is. So don't escalate the situation with

sarcasm, condescension or, worse, yelling.

- If your son is shouting, shaking, sweating, has clenched fists or shows other signs of being in fight or flight mode, walk away.
- Seek professional help for your son from a psychologist or mental health professional. It is not uncommon for young men to minimise, justify or deny that they have used violence, and they will often resort to victim blaming. They need help to learn to identify and deal with emotions, resolve conflict and self-soothe.
- You may also seek help from a family support service. All family members need support to deal with the violent adolescent's behaviour, and having a strong connection makes a vital difference to outcomes at this stage of development.
- Call 000 if anyone is in immediate danger.

Start with your GP or a family support service in your area. Criminal justice responses should be a last resort and are usually only used by families who fear for the safety of other family members or are concerned that their son risks negative personal, academic or employment outcomes.

WHAT CAN THE POLICE DO?

While most parents are extremely reluctant or apprehensive about calling the police, the bottom line is that they may be able to provide assistance and protection when you need it the most. For example:

- It sends a message to your son that his behaviour constitutes assault, that it is illegal and that you will not accept it.
- It may stop the abuse long enough for you and/or other members of your family to be removed to a place of safety.
- It can give you time to obtain a family violence intervention order that protects you from emotional, physical, sexual or financial abuse.
- The police can arrest your son for hurting you or violating a family violence intervention order.
- The police will document the abuse, including taking photos of any injuries and obtaining witness statements.

INTERVENTION ORDERS

Any family member can apply for a family violence intervention order at the local Magistrates' Court. An interim order is available if you require immediate protection. If you have other children and you fear for their safety, they can be included in the application. The person the intervention order will protect is called the 'affected family member' or the 'protected person'. The person the intervention order is made against is called 'the respondent'. Intervention orders include specific stipulations to stop the respondent from using violence against the protected person or people. If the respondent fails to comply with the conditions of an intervention order, the police can, and very often will, charge them with a criminal offence.

Chapter 21

Toxic intimate relationships

As parents, you lose the capacity to influence the social choices children make pretty much from the moment they hit high school. Yes, you can attempt to 'encourage' connections through extracurricular activities (where you get involved in coaching or transporting the kids, or socialising with the other parents). But your kids know who they like (even if they can't explain why) and will gravitate towards them, regardless of what you think, say or do. The same, of course, goes for romantic/intimate relationships.

For Prince Boofheads, choosing a mate tends to be on the basis of looks, socio-economic status or other traits associated with superiority. They engage only superficially in their intimate relationships, rather than establishing an authentic, emotional bond. When boys are young, this way of relating isn't uncommon, but it's shallow and can become problematic in later years.

When asked in therapy about friendships, one young Prince Boofhead said, 'I don't worry about whether or not someone is a legitimate friend. It's all a transaction anyway: they get something, you get something – leave it at that.' This means that the success of the relationship hinges on external factors (such as appearance, connections and current perceived success) rather than internal, emotional fulfilment. And as soon as one of those external factors changes, he is likely to trade in his partner for a new model.

KEY FEATURES OF TOXIC RELATIONSHIPS

- Prince Boofhead will initially use incredible charm to engage his partner, putting her or him on a pedestal and making them feel worshipped and loved. His partner will be quite besotted by the attention and doting behaviour.
- Boofhead will often choose a partner who is slightly less dominant than he is, enabling him to do what he wants without too much resistance. He may also choose a partner who is emotionally less stable because this allows him to be in control. This can also lead to an emotionally volatile basis for a relationship.
- To gain or maintain power in the relationship, Boofhead will begin to pick faults and imperfections in his partner. This will tap into his partner's insecurity and see them trying to 'be good enough' to win back Boofhead's initial affection.
- In times of frustration, or in the context of jealousy, or when Boofhead isn't getting what he wants, he may become aggressive, manipulative, threatening,

intimidating, coercive and, occasionally, violent. These patterns of behaviour wreak havoc on the wellbeing of Boofhead's partner.

- If Boofhead has mental health and/or substance abuse issues, this increases the intensity of relationship difficulties.
- Boofhead will not consider his partner's feelings when he decides to discard the relationship (usually because he is not reaping the benefits he expected, or someone better comes along).

MODELLING RESPECTFUL RELATIONSHIPS

Unbeknownst to him, Prince Boofhead will typically recreate the same pattern of interacting with a partner that he learned from interacting with the first female figure in his life (usually his mother). This is due in part to choosing a relationship that on some level feels psychologically familiar (there's nothing weird about this, of course – this is a way of relating that has long been ingrained). In fact, it can become so automatic for some young men that it translates into the ways they perceive and interact with other women who come and go in their lives.

Parents teach their sons what to expect from women, and how to respect women. If boys become young men who have, over time, systematically devalued or even discarded their mothers, or seen their own fathers do the same, you'll likely witness a similar pattern emerge with Prince Boofhead and his chosen partners.

Many of the tips from other chapters will help you guide Prince Boofhead to avoid engaging in these toxic relationships. However, if things feel like they are out of control, it may be worth considering getting some help from a psychologist or other mental health professional. This may help to shift the attitudes he may hold about the value of relationships. See chapter 24 for more details.

Chapter 22

Depression

Anyone who has lived with teenagers for even a nano-second knows that they can be extremely volatile. One moment they are whistling and the next they can be sullen, furious or irritable.

For teenage boys, low moods may last for a few minutes, hours or days, and may result from some loss or disappointment in life, or for no apparent reason at all. However, when a young man displays a pervasive sense of despair that lasts longer than two weeks and interferes with his friendships and daily activities, parents must consider the possibility of a looming depressive illness.

Depression is much more than sadness – it is an illness that destroys rational thinking processes, extinguishes hope and distorts moods. It causes a young man to lose interest in most of his usual activities and, in some cases, can take away his desire to live. The normal stresses of life (friends, school, work and so on) can seem unbearable for someone suffering depression. Indeed, the strain of trying to pretend that 'nothing is wrong' can exacerbate the illness. It can also mean he will resort to self-medication with alcohol and other illicit drugs that in turn may result in a substance abuse disorder, academic problems and sometimes legal problems.

Depression can occur by itself, but is usually associated with other mental disorders, such as generalised anxiety disorder, panic disorder, obsessive compulsive disorder, anorexia, self-harm, bipolar disorder and psychosis. Research indicates a link between untreated anxiety in primary school and the development of depression in high school.

Estimated rates of major depressive disorder among teenagers aged 12–17 in the 2015 Child and Adolescent Survey of Mental Health and Wellbeing were 4.3 per cent of males and 5.8 per cent of females. The key message from organisations like beyondblue is that untreated depression can kill. Sadly, research suggests that many people with depression report delays of 5–15 years before they receive treatment and care. This is particularly disastrous, as there is good peer-reviewed evidence that early diagnosis and prompt treatment are associated with much more favourable outcomes.

So where does this all start? And how do we know if our sons are at risk?

WHAT CAUSES DEPRESSION?

Rather than looking for causes, it's more helpful to talk in terms of the balance of risk and protective factors. There are both internal (personal and genetic) and external (environmental and experiential) risk factors that affect whether or not a young person will experience depression. Conversely, there are also important protective factors that can mitigate these risks.

RISK FACTORS

Internal risk factors include:

- having an underlying genetic predisposition for depression (research shows that teenagers with a depressed parent have a 40 per cent chance of experiencing depression by the age of 20, and a 60 per cent chance by the age of 25; however, this risk is reduced if certain protective factors are in place)
- having a pessimistic personality
- having poor interpersonal skills coupled with negative thought processes.

External risk factors include experiencing:

- child physical or sexual abuse
- problems at school (e.g. not coping with the academic workload, not fitting in, being bullied)
- unresolved grief over the death of a parent, sibling or close friend
- ongoing conflict or violence at home or in the community
- a relationship breakup
- family separation or divorce
- drug and/or alcohol abuse
- chronic illness or injury
- chronic poverty.

All of these risk factors may create difficulties for adolescents already negotiating changing relationships with peers and families, searching for autonomy while trying to fit in, and simultaneously trying to succeed in a competitive academic and social environment. In short, as the academic Dr Jane Burns wrote in the *Medical Journal of Australia*, 'cumulative adverse experiences, including negative life events and early childhood adversity, together with parental depression and/or non-supportive school or familial environments, all place young people at risk for developing depression.'

PROTECTIVE FACTORS

But the good news is that risk factors can be offset by protective factors such as:
* social connectedness
* fulfilment and life satisfaction
* emotional resilience.

Dr Martin Seligman, the 'father' of positive psychology, suggests that if we can teach children aged 10–12 optimistic thinking, we can halve the rates of depression and anxiety as they go through adolescence.

SIGNS AND SYMPTOMS OF DEPRESSION IN TEENAGE BOYS

Because most young men have mood swings from time to time, are often reluctant to share thoughts and feelings with adult carers, are highly sensitive to control and often don't have the emotional vocabulary to convey how they are feeling, it can be challenging to work out if they are depressed.

Parents should look for a cluster of symptoms that extend over a few weeks or more:

- Persistent sadness and bouts of crying
- Gloomy and dark statements (direct and indirect) that they feel worthless, self-critical, pessimistic about their future or don't want to continue living
- Loss of interest in friends and usual pleasurable activities
- Loss of appetite (or overeating)
- Insomnia (or hypersomnia)
- Decline in academic performance
- Increased irritability, anger or hostility
- Indecisiveness
- Tiredness and lack of motivation (or restlessness, agitation)
- Uncharacteristic/risky behaviours such as drug and alcohol misuse, stealing, inappropriate sexual contacts, reckless driving or bullying
- Deliberate self-harm

Often young people with depression also experience anxiety at the same time, which can cause physical symptoms like pain, a pounding heart or stomach cramps.

DIAGNOSING AND TREATING DEPRESSION

If you suspect your son may be depressed, the first step is to make an appointment with a GP. Your doctor can then refer your son to a psychiatrist or psychologist if necessary.

While there is no blood test for depression, the Kessler 10 (K10) checklist is widely suggested as a straightforward measure of psychological distress and a way of assessing the level of success of treatment for common mental health disorders. This is a questionnaire that parents can get their teenagers to complete, and that GPs will understand if you discuss the results with them – taking the results of a K10 to an appointment is a great start. The K10 is available from the beyondblue website.

There are now many ways to treat depression, including talking therapies (such as counselling, cognitive behavioural therapy and psychotherapy) and antidepressant medication. If the burden of the disease is severe (e.g. it involves self-harm, withdrawal from friends, family conflict or school refusal), then a combination of medication and talking therapies will be used.

Supportive counselling can help ease the pain of depression and address the feelings of hopelessness that accompany the illness. In addition, cognitive behavioural therapy may help your son to:

- recognise which life problems are critical and which are less so
- develop positive life goals
- identify unhelpful beliefs and unrealistic expectations, and replace them with more adaptive cognitions
- develop a more positive self-assessment.

HELPING YOUR SON RECOVER FROM DEPRESSION

After treatment for depression, most teenagers get back to normal life quite quickly. However, if another adverse life event comes along and derails them from completing their developmental tasks, they can quite easily slip back into depression. Relapse rates for depressed teenagers can be as high as 50–70 per cent, and there is always a possibility of it recurring later in life.

To reduce the chances of a relapse, there are many things your son can do. The best approach is to build on protective factors, such as positive social relationships, adequate sleep and exercise, a healthy diet and engaging in activities that give him a sense of purpose and fulfilment.

Exercise

According to beyondblue, keeping active is a key strategy in managing depression. They cite research showing that regular physical activity significantly reduces the risk of people developing depression. Regular aerobics and strength training at a light or moderate intensity, such as riding a bike, jogging or walking, can result in up to a 50 per cent reduction in symptoms of depression and anxiety.

Sleep

An inability to sleep, or insomnia, is one of the signs of depression. (A small percentage of depressed people oversleep or sleep too much – this is called hypersomnia.) Lack of sleep alone cannot cause depression, but it does exacerbate it. Lack of sleep caused by another medical illness or by personal problems can make depression worse. An inability to sleep that lasts over a long period of time is also an important clue that someone might be depressed. See chapter 11 for more detail on improving teenage sleep.

Evidence suggests that people with insomnia have a ten-fold risk of developing depression compared with those who sleep well. Insomnia symptoms include difficulty falling asleep (sleep onset insomnia), difficulty staying asleep (sleep maintenance insomnia), unrefreshing sleep and daytime sleepiness. Establishing a good sleep/wake routine that includes regular exercise and early daylight exposure will help improve a teenager's mood, energy and general health and wellbeing, as well as helping him sleep better at night.

Keep talking

Talking about depression as an illness ensures that we de-stigmatise it. If there is a family history, then frank, open conversations about increased risk and discussions of protective factors are crucial. If appropriate, discuss with your son what the early signs of depression are so that he is more vigilant to its recurrence. Also, encourage him to talk through his problems with a trusted adult. If possible, have him keep in touch with a therapist for a few months after he is feeling better.

SUICIDE

Do not shy away from discussing the subject of suicide with your son. Teachable moments arise every day either through the media or the experiences of families or friends. Any suicide to which your son is exposed – however tangentially – needs to be reframed as the outcome of a mental illness (most often depression).

The challenge for all parents of boys is to be sufficiently tuned in to their psychology to notice the slightest warning signs and to act quickly, before he elects, as so many do, to retreat to his room and communicate with no-one.

Richard was just 17 years old when he took his life. The eldest of three children, he grew up in a loving family in a normal house in a normal suburb. Yet his family now lives with the agonising question of what, if anything, they could have done to prevent the devastating loss.

Looking back, Richard did show signs of depression. He reported feelings of sadness and hopelessness to his friends (who weren't really sure what to do about it), and was irritable, hostile and, at times, angry towards his family over the six weeks before his death. His parents described him as being tearful, and say that he withdrew from friends and family and lost interest in the activities that he used to enjoy, such as swimming and football. His mother noticed marked changes in his eating and sleeping habits. He attended school but became progressively more and more negative about it, mainly because he had difficulty concentrating and felt restless and agitated in class. One of his friends later said that Richard had told him that he hated everything except listening to rap music.

Despite his inner turmoil, Richard made an

effort to maintain an outwardly brave face. But this proved futile, and he finally reached a point where he no longer found anything interesting, enjoyable or worthwhile. Over the last few weeks of his life, every thought, word and movement had become an effort. Unbeknownst to those who loved him, his depressed brain did little more than torment him with a dreary litany of his inadequacies and shortcomings, taunting him with the desperate hopelessness of it all.

There were also significant risk factors at play that indicated Richard was prone to depression. First, there was a history of depression on both sides of the family, which significantly ratchets up the chances for the next generation. Second, there had been a major change in the family when, four years earlier, his parents had undergone a nasty separation.

With the benefit of hindsight, it is almost certain that Richard was suffering from rapid onset unipolar depression, a severe illness that distorted his moods and led to uncharacteristic behaviour. Without the reinforcements afforded by antidepressant medication, exercise, diet and cognitive behavioural therapy, thoughts of death became his constant companion. Yet right up until the end he gave few outward signs, other than complaining to his friends of feeling sad and tired. For Richard, dying was the only release from the unbearable misery and overwhelming sense of inadequacy and blackness that surrounded him.

So what might have saved Richard? What could his

loving family have done to try and prevent this tragic outcome? In an ideal world, his family would have learned from their own experiences with depression and taken him to the family doctor he'd been seeing since birth. The doctor, knowing the family history of depression, would have given him a thorough and considered assessment, and referred him to a psychiatrist who would have ensured he received regular counselling, took his medication and attended frequent check-ups. His parents would have talked openly about depression with him, so that he did not feel the awful burden of having to endure the disease alone. And they would have directed him to user-friendly psycho-education in the form of apps, websites and fact sheets to read when he could concentrate. But that is an ideal world.

Chapter 23
Anxiety

Everyone feels worried or afraid sometimes, and we're all familiar with the elevated heart rate, quickened breathing, sweating and other physical reactions that accompany our fear. This fight or flight response is a completely normal reaction to perceived danger that we evolved to help improve our chances of survival. However, for some people, this stress response is activated so powerfully and so frequently that it interferes with their ability to cope with everyday life. Some experience panic attacks, where the physical reactions are so overwhelming that they feel they are having a heart attack, a brain haemorrhage or are dying.

There are many different kinds of anxiety disorders, including generalised anxiety disorder (GAD), where the worry is not specific to any one thing but is a general feeling of foreboding; social anxiety disorder (a fear of being humiliated or embarrassed in public); panic disorder (a fear of having panic attacks); agoraphobia (a fear of being in a situation from which escape might be difficult or embarrassing if you have a panic attack); specific phobias (an intense and ongoing fear of particular objects or situations such as flying, lifts or mice); obsessive compulsive disorder (OCD), which involves repetitive thoughts and compulsive acts you use to try to calm your anxiety, like checking things or counting things; and post-traumatic stress disorder (PTSD), which involves upsetting memories, flashbacks, nightmares and insomnia triggered by an accident, sexual assault or other major traumatic event.

According to statistics from the 2015 Child and Adolescent Survey of Mental Health and Wellbeing, 7 per cent of young people aged 12–17 years have one or more anxiety disorders, with social phobia, separation anxiety disorder and generalised anxiety disorder being the most common.

RISK FACTORS FOR ANXIETY

As with depression, anxiety disorders arise from a combination of genetic and environmental factors. A history of anxiety within your family increases the chances that your offspring may develop an anxiety disorder, as do stressful events such as a relationship break-up, family violence, ongoing bullying at school, sexual abuse, the death of a close friend or family member, or being involved in an accident, natural disaster or war.

Anxiety is more common in adolescents living in families with lower levels of income, education and employment and with poorer family functioning. Of children or adolescents living in families with one parent or carer, 9 per cent had separation anxiety disorder compared with

2.7 per cent in original (intact) families – considerably higher than other types of anxiety. Anxiety disorders are also more common for children or adolescents living outside of capital cities.

SIGNS AND SYMPTOMS OF ANXIETY IN TEENAGE BOYS

Central features of anxiety include:
- racing negative thoughts about future events
- difficulty concentrating
- feeling impatient and irritable (like things are too slow)
- feeling on edge (like something bad is about to happen)
- trouble falling asleep and staying asleep.

Physical signs sometimes also include:
- a racing heart or tight chest
- sweating, blushing or feeling hot
- fast, shallow breathing or shortness of breath
- dizziness or headaches
- tingling or numbness
- a dry mouth or difficulty swallowing
- stomach pain or nausea.

Although the anxiety disorders have different symptoms, they all tend to make the teenager withdraw into themselves in an attempt to avoid situations or objects that trigger the anxiety. In early adolescence they may avoid social interaction with their peers and even with their family. In later adolescence, they may avoid getting involved in relationships because they fear rejection, and can develop serious self-esteem problems. Untreated, such young people will struggle at school and are less likely to achieve their educational potential, which in turn affects their job prospects. Teenagers with untreated anxiety in particular are likely to suffer co-existing conditions such as eating disorders, depression and drug and alcohol problems. But the problem affects entire families. As with any case of illness, siblings may be resentful of the attention the sufferer is getting.

Contrary to popular belief, these adolescents aren't overindulged hypochondriacs. They are suffering a mental disorder that can make their lives a living hell.

DIAGNOSING AND TREATING ANXIETY

For parents, it can be tricky to work out the difference between normal teenage behaviour and the signs of a developing anxiety disorder. If your son appears unhappy, stressed, is avoiding social situations, refusing to go to school or displaying obsessive and compulsive behaviours (such as frequent showering or washing hands, wiping doorknobs, counting food, etc.), then you must act now. The earlier he seeks help the better, and your first port of call should be a visit to the doctor.

The most common form of treatment for anxiety is cognitive behavioural therapy (CBT), usually undertaken with a psychologist trained in this method, although some psychiatrists also offer this type of therapy. In some cases medication may be prescribed as a short-term measure, although research suggests that CBT is much more effective than medication in managing anxiety disorders in the long term.

HELPING YOUR SON COPE WITH ANXIETY

Stress is part of life. Sometimes shit just happens and there's nothing we can do about it. Stress reduction is not about trying to control, limit or prevent things from going wrong, but about changing the way we react when they don't go according to plan.

To manage anxiety, your son needs to activate his body's natural relaxation response – the opposite of the fight or fight response. It is a physical state of profound rest that relaxes muscles, slows breathing and heart rate, and increases blood flow to the brain. And the easiest way to activate this response? Diaphragmatic breathing. The diaphragm is the muscle below your lungs that, when contracted, allows the lungs to completely fill. Pushing your stomach out contracts this muscle (that's why it's also called belly breathing). It is thought that diaphragmatic breathing stimulates the vagus nerve, which supplies parasympathetic fibres to the rest of the body.

Normally, when we are in a stressful situation we begin to take quick, shallow breaths – our chests and shoulders moving up and down. This, in turn, increases our stress level. Recognising the signs of stress and taking deep breaths that move our diaphragm and belly up and down can immediately calm us down and allow us to think through the situation.

Use technology to manage anxiety

ReachOut Worrytime is a smartphone app that helps young people to contain their worry to designated periods, thereby freeing up their mind for other activities. This is known as stimulus control training and is a standard technique of cognitive behavioural therapy with proven results. The app gives him a place to 'store' his worries and alert him to when it's time to think about them. When a worry no longer matters to him, he can ditch it and move on.

ReachOut Breathe is one of the world's first wellbeing apps specifically designed for Apple Watch, and it is also available for iPhone. Using simple visuals, the app helps people reduce the physical symptoms of stress and anxiety by slowing down their heart rate to increase feelings of calmness in their body. The iPhone version also utilises biofeedback to measure heart rate so that users can track changes in real time.

The use of technology to manage wellbeing will change over time and many new apps, biometric devices and web-based programs will appear. Parents must resist the temptation to dismiss these innovations, since many have been found to have scientific validity in helping young people change worrying behaviours including obsessive-compulsive disorder, self-harm and substance abuse.

Chapter 24

Seeking professional help

We all want our sons to be able to successfully navigate adult life – to engage with people in the workforce, to see life as an exercise in cooperation rather than competition, and to experience an intimate relationship as more than a 'transaction'. We also want our boys to be able to develop the resilience required to cope with life's inevitable setbacks, so that a simple disappointment doesn't blow out into a totally derailing catastrophe. In short, we want to make sure our boys are equipped to manage all areas of their lives now and into the future.

However, as we have seen, some boys (due to a mix of genetic disposition and environmental factors), suffer from anxiety, depression, anger issues or addiction – all of which require parents to seek professional help.

It can be pretty tough to come to terms with the possibility that you need another person to help you. It may feel like you're finding a psychologist to take on a pseudo-parenting role for your child. This doesn't mean you have failed as a parent. All it means is that you are courageous enough to enlist some external help for a certain amount of time. Ultimately, such an influence could improve the way your son feels about himself and, importantly, the interactions he has with all other people in his life.

But, let's be completely frank. Therapy wouldn't just be for Prince Boofhead. As I have said, the environment has a huge amount to do with the development of his attitudes and behaviours, and therapy would also aim to empower you with alternative perspectives and strategies for parenting.

The cornerstone of my work is that beliefs, attitudes and behaviours can be changed. Modern cognitive behavioural therapists, of which I am one, posit that you cannot have a feeling (such as anger) without first having a thought or belief that triggered it. Furthermore, the way we think about and interpret our experiences is richly influenced by prior experiences that shape our often deeply held beliefs. If you can encourage your son to see a therapist (and model doing so yourself), you can begin to shift attitudes that he may hold about the value of relationships.

> Devlin strides into the therapist's room and sits down with his legs wide apart. He combs his hair with one hand while checking his reflection in the window. Then, while casually taking in the surroundings, his eyes come to rest on the therapist with a steady, steely gaze – as if to say 'let the games begin'.
> Therapist: So Devlin, you've mentioned that your mother finds it extremely difficult to say sorry.

Devlin: Yes. That's right.

Therapist: Why do you think it's so difficult for her to say sorry?

Devlin: She can't stand the idea of being seen as wrong or weak.

Therapist: Do you think that someone who says sorry is weak, or could they actually be confident?

Devlin: Um . . . oh, both.

Therapist: In what way?

Devlin: I'm not really sure.

Therapist: Is someone who can say sorry confident because they can acknowledge a minor error, without feeling like it has somehow dented their value or self-worth? You know, acknowledging their mistake doesn't have to define them as a failure or weak in that moment. Better still, they can accept the situation, and then move on without the disappointment washing them out to sea.

Devlin: I guess so. I hadn't thought about it like that.

The therapist knows only too well that people find it much easier to identify behaviours in others than in themselves. By opening the discussion with his mother's alleged issues with vulnerability, the therapist opens up the possibility that Devlin may challenge his own negative beliefs about vulnerability, and hopefully be a little less self-critical the next time he makes a mistake.

THE VALUE OF THERAPY

The therapeutic alliance is an important one, because

unlike family (who are perceived as unconditional supporters) the therapist can potentially become someone Prince Boofhead learns to respect. This could have flow-on effects for how he comes to interact with others outside of therapy.

The therapeutic process can help him shift his perception of relationships as 'transactions' to safe and supportive connections that involve positive emotions. The therapist can also ask him challenging questions about himself, his relationships and the direction of his life without the emotional charge that accompanies such questions from his parents.

Therapy can also assist mothers and fathers to develop new strategies around parenting so that they can positively enable their boys.

GETTING THEM THROUGH THE DOOR

One of the biggest challenges parents can face when encouraging their boys to consider therapy is how to get them through the door. I usually encourage parents of these types of boys – in fact, any child that may not want to come and see a psychologist (which is many of them) – to tell their child that he will be putting the therapist to the test, rather than the other way around. This appeals to their sense of superiority (their belief, at this stage, that no-one is smart enough to help them) and their conviction that they don't need it anyway. In this way there's an illusion of choice – that it's up to them to determine whether they feel comfortable and safe with the interaction and, that if they don't, they can find a different therapist.

The collaborative relationship between the therapist and client is the key to the process of change. When they agree on shared goals and work on them together, they establish a rapport built upon trust, acceptance and empathy. The way Prince Boofhead sees himself and those around him may shift and he will begin to enjoy mutually beneficial relationships.

WHAT IF YOU CAN'T AFFORD A PSYCHOLOGIST?

If you don't have private medical insurance, your doctor can arrange a GP mental health treatment plan with Medicare, where you will be able to access the services of a psychologist or clinical psychologist for a total of 10 sessions per calendar year and pay only the gap between their fee and the current Medicare rebate. If the gap is still unmanageable (and your family has a Health Care Card) it is worth asking the psychologist if they might consider lowering the gap. The important thing is that you find a way to get the help you and your son needs.

Resources

adf.org.au

The Alcohol and Drug Foundation is a nationwide organisa-
tion committed to preventing alcohol and other drug harms
in Australia. It has excellent resources for young people,
parents and the broader community.

theothertalk.org.au

This website offers specific information for parents who want
to talk to their kids about drug and alcohol use.

sharc.org.au/program/family-drug-help/

Family Drug Help provides a specialist service to support
family members and friends who are concerned about a loved
one's alcohol and other drug use.

strongbonds.jss.org.au

Strong Bonds is run by Jesuit Social Services and offers useful
information to help you support your young person through
hard times, so that you can keep making a difference to their
health and wellbeing.

ysas.org.au

The Youth Support and Advocacy Service is a Victorian

not-for-profit agency dedicated to providing resources and support for young people affected by drugs, alcohol and mental health issues.

hellosundaymorning.org

This website offers online support and apps to help people moderate their drinking.

healthyfamilies.beyondblue.org.au/age-13

This website provides information on raising resilient young people and common mental health problems.

headspace.org.au

This is the website for the national youth mental health foundation dedicated to improving the wellbeing of young people.

cyh.com

This website provides information for parents and teenagers on health and wellbeing.

raisingchildren.net.au/teens/teens.html

The Raising Children Network has information and tips on raising healthy teenagers.

commonsensemedia.org

Common Sense Media improves the lives of kids and families by providing independent reviews, age ratings andother information about all types of media.

Acknowledgements

Thank you to Miriam and Charlotte for their invaluable advice and assistance in writing this book, as well as to publisher Ali Watts, editor Amanda Martin and the rest of the team at Penguin.

Michael would like to thank all the young men and their families who have shared their journeys with him over the years and his wife, Therese, with whom he first shared and understood the challenges and delights of parenting boys.

Elly would like to thank the Year 8 crew for keeping her up to date and endlessly amused. Thanks also to Genevieve and Emily for reviewing the draft and providing great feedback on raising teenage boys.

Index

the
PRINCESS
BITCHFACE
SYNDROME 2.0

Surviving
adolescent
girls

MICHAEL CARR-GREGG
and ELLY ROBINSON

If you feel like you're losing control when it comes
to parenting your daughter, it's time to grab back
the reins with this phenomenal Australian bestseller –
over 100 000 copies sold.